WILDERNESS PREDATORS OF THE ROCKIES

The Bond between Predator and Prey

Mike Lapinski

FALCON GUIDE®

GUILFORD, CONNECTICUT
HELENA, MONTANA

AN IMPRINT OF THE GLOBE PEQUOT PRESS

Text design: Nancy Freeborn
Photos are by Mike Lapinski except where otherwise noted.

Library of Congress Cataloging-in-Publication Data
Lapinski, Michael.
  Wilderness predators of the Rockies : the bond between predator and prey / Mike Lapinski.—1st ed.
    p. cm.
  Includes bibliographical references.
  ISBN 0-7627-3537-6 (alk. paper)
  1. Predatory animals—Ecology—Rocky Mountains. I. Title.
  QL758.L37 2006
  591.5'3'0978—dc22

                                                            2005016664

Manufactured in the United States of America
First Edition/First Printing

To buy books in quantity for corporate use
or incentives, call **(800) 962–0973, ext. 4551,**
or e-mail **premiums@GlobePequot.com.**

THIS BOOK IS DEDICATED TO AGGIE
who encourages me to find myself in the wilderness
and awaits my return.

An elk at the base of the Mission Mountains in Montana

CONTENTS

Acknowledgments vi

Introduction 1

The Wilderness Life Cycle 3

The Critical Prey Base 10

The Grizzly Bear 22

The Black Bear 38

The Wolf 53

The Mountain Coyote 71

The Mountain Lion 89

The Lynx 104

The Bobcat 117

The Wolverine 128

The Fisher 142

The Marten 153

The Ermine 164

Ghost Predators of the Southern Rockies 175

Conclusion 196

Bibliography 200

About the Author 202

ACKNOWLEDGMENTS

Much of this book is the result of my personal experiences and observations as I trekked through the Rocky Mountain wilderness. However, I would like to thank Bill Van Pelt, nongame wildlife specialist for the Arizona Department of Wildlife, who furnished much information about the exciting migration of the jaguar into Arizona and New Mexico.

Anyone who is interested in the natural world should strive to obtain a copy of Ernest Seton's four-volume *Lives of Game Animals*. This collection, though not always easily available, is a treasure trove of how the natural world functions. Written almost a century ago, this collection of books has been my inspiration to delve deeper into the ways of wilderness predators than the superficial jottings of an antiseptic biology book.

INTRODUCTION

This book is brimming with fascinating information about those legendary predators that inhabit the Rocky Mountains. Stretching for three thousand miles from northeastern British Columbia to New Mexico, and intermittently to northern Mexico, the Rockies form a vast wilderness of high, rugged peaks and vast coniferous forests that harbor the massive grizzly and black bear, the gray wolf, the mountain lion, lynx, bobcat, mountain coyote, wolverine, fisher, marten, and ermine. Adding to this impressive list is the exciting news that in recent years the mighty jaguar, the largest cat in the western hemisphere, has reappeared in the southern Rockies.

Every page of *Wilderness Predators of the Rockies* offers newly discovered facts and insights concerning each predator's surprising fragility and resilience, as its tumultuous life-and-death struggles unfold in the never-ending cycle of nature. Chapters about a single species end with a reference section with the following information: *Species Description, Habitat, Range and Population,* and *Mating.*

I have spent more than three decades roaming through some of the remotest areas of the Rockies and observing these predators. I've watched the gray wolf change in the blink of an eye from a playful canine to a deadly killer. I've stared down, trembling, from atop a hastily climbed tree into the smoldering eyes of a grizzly; had the unnerving experience of being followed by a mountain lion along a trail at dusk; and felt the eyes of the jaguar burning into my back as I pushed through a juniper/pinion forest in Arizona.

I'm not alone in my love of the Rocky Mountain wilderness and its predators. With increasing frequency nature lovers seek a fuller understanding of these awesome predators of legend and myth. Every spring, hundreds of ecotourists and nature lovers, from bankers to housewives, stand shoulder to shoulder in bone-chilling rain to catch a glimpse of a Yellowstone wolf or a surly grizzly bear.

It is gratifying to hear the rousing cheers that emanate from this smorgasbord of humanity when a pack of wolves or a roaming grizzly takes down an elk or a bison. Their gleeful shrieks harken us back to an earlier age when humans struggled desperately, valiantly, to rise from the status of easy prey to supreme predator. For in watching such spectacles, we humans are reminded that we also are predators and therefore identify with the predator world.

Do you live far from the haunts of the taciturn wolf or surly grizzly? Is your life structured by demands that keep you from these hallowed places deep within the bosom of the Rockies? If so, I'll be your eyes and ears until you get there.

In writing this book, it is my heartfelt desire that these awesome beasts of claw and fang become much more to you than mere textbook specimens. Ultimately, my hope is that you will feel an affection, and a kinship, for every beast from predator to prey.

Disclaimer

Though at times I have occasionally observed wild animals at close range as I moved through the wilderness while tracking them to learn their habits, a close encounter should be avoided. All wild animals are potentially dangerous and should never be approached but instead be viewed at a safe distance to avoid stressing them and triggering a defensive, aggressive reaction.

THE WILDERNESS LIFE CYCLE

A Wilderness Experience

At dawn the treasure of wilderness lies hidden behind a soft mist. It tantalizes and teases, a vague timbered ridge here, the silhouette of an animal there. Slowly, as if heralding a great rediscovery, the morning sun burns through the fog, splashing soft golden rays upon a pristine land stretching before the eyes, fresh and newly washed.

Wildflowers carpet the alpine meadows in soft, multicolored hues. Granite mountains rise skyward like silent, brooding sentinels, protecting their treasures below. Even in summer snowfields cling to the sheer rock walls above, releasing a steady gush of pure, ice-cold water to nourish the countless meandering streams below.

And like jewels on a crown, deer and elk in scattered herds feed on the lush meadow grasses. On a distant ridge a lone gray wolf emerges from a stand of fir trees, and all the elk stop to watch until it trots out of sight. Along the far edge of the meadow, a grizzly bear ambles along, stopping occasionally to dig for roots and ground squirrels. Most of the fleet-footed elk ignore the bear and continue feeding, but there always seems to be one elk watching. Far above, a wolverine lopes along, hungrily following the trail of a few windblown molecules of odor that have wafted forth in the morning breeze from a winter-killed bighorn sheep carcass a half mile away.

But wilderness pleases far more than just the visual senses. The tantalizing aroma of fresh earth, decaying wood, and ferns mixes with the pungent aroma of low-bush huckleberries and the heady fragrance of pine and spruce. You breathe differently up here in the wilderness. It makes you want to pull in slowly, deeply through your nose, just in case you may have missed something.

Though there is peace and solitude up here, it's seldom a haunting silence. Crows and ravens send forth a cacophony of calls as they converse in their own language. A furry little pica sits atop a rock outcrop and scolds you for intruding upon its domain. Off in the distance coyotes yip back and forth at each other but are silenced by the ominous howls of wolves. A nearby black bear noisily gobbles dew-kissed huckleberries, and cow elk emit their musical, nasal calls.

You sit and take in this special place, luxuriating in the peaceful transforming of your soul from the urban to the natural. Unfortunately, the time in man's development has passed when you can stay up here forever. Eventually, you must return to the asphalt and concrete, but you take one last look, one last breath, one last listen to the natural world before you hurry down the trail to your vehicle. The wilderness experience is about to end, but you now possess a treasure in your mind, heart, and soul to take back and revisit whenever it gets to be too much down there. It's enough to tide you over until the next time.

Wilderness Defined

Wilderness is easier to designate than it is to define. Webster's dictionary definition of wilderness is ludicrous: a land of wild and waste, uncivilized and uninhabited. Small wonder we of the higher order of primates have such difficulty stewarding the natural world.

Essentially, any natural land that remains free from the encroachment of civilization and maintains its predator/prey base relatively intact can be considered wilderness, even if it has not been officially designated as a wilderness area by the federal government.

The Wilderness Life Cycle

Wilderness is not just a place; it's a function, a finely tuned natural state where every blade of grass, bush, tree, insect, bird, and mammal plays a role in making nature's life cycle appear clean and flawless. In this state of perfection, no single entity commands more respect or importance than another.

As such, a tiny windblown grass seed is just as important as the mighty grizzly bear because when the seed takes root and flourishes, the hoary marmot snips its succulent shoots and grows fat just before the grizzly comes along in late summer and digs it from its den. By eating the marmot that ate the grass that grew from the tiny seed, the grizzly is sustained through hibernation. But before the great bear takes its long winter's nap, it voids its bowels onto a tiny windblown seed, thereby providing fertilizer for the cycle to repeat next spring.

In this one small instance, we see the perfect cycle of nature revolving. But in the wilderness there are hundreds, thousands, millions, billions of these microecosystems unfolding separately, yet simultaneously. The result is a pristine land functioning with a wondrous simplicity and efficiency. But this perfection comes at a price.

The Price of Perfection

Ancient scriptures prophesize of a future time of peace in the world, when avarice and death will be replaced with harmony and tranquility—an age when the lion will lie down with the lamb. We all look forward to that day. In the meantime the lion eats the lamb.

And yet, this bittersweet relationship between predator and prey is a conundrum because it never culminates as a total victory, with the predators finally eating all the prey, or the prey escaping long enough to starve off the predators. Instead, it has an ebb and flow of surpluses and deficiencies; when viewed as an overall harmonious system, the predator/prey relationship is forever renewable.

The only problem with this red-stained equation is occasional human interference. We live in a democratic society where all humans and, to some degree, animals have rights. A strong man has no right to prey upon a frail woman or child. Human predators are dealt with harshly, even put to death in some cases.

Yet in the natural world the weak, the sick, the young, and the unlucky are killed by those who are bigger, stronger, faster. It is, for want of a better phrase, the law of the jungle. Still, it sticks in the craw of civilized man and often results in human intrusion into nature's plan that produces more carnage than the seemingly evil natural scheme.

A good example was an incident related to me by two hikers whom I'd met on a backcountry trail in western Montana. In breathless dialogue they related how they'd just "saved" a calf elk from a mountain lion.

The two hikers had stopped at a bend in the trail overlooking a meadow below. A cow and calf elk were feeding 200 yards away along the edge of a rock bluff. Suddenly, a smallish mountain lion appeared, stalking to within 50 yards of the elk before the frantic hikers began yelling and throwing rocks. The lion whirled and stood uncertainly while the cow and calf elk escaped into the timber. The cat finally skulked back into the brush.

The hikers were rather nonplused when I mentioned that it might have been for the best if the lion had killed the calf elk. They gave me the most absurd look before continuing on their way, anxious to retell the story about how they'd saved the elk from the lion.

The consequences of this human interference with nature's cycle carried tremendously damaging potential. Because the lion was small, it was probably a female with kittens nearby, and it was desperately trying to find food to nourish its body and provide milk for the kits. Quite possibly, those kittens died of starvation.

Another sidelight to this incident appeared in the local newspaper a week later, relating how a female lion had been shot after it stalked and killed a dog in the backyard of a country home 10 miles away. I often wonder if it had been the same female, milkless and emaciated, who'd been driven near-mad watching her squealing kittens slowly wither.

And what about the elk? Was that calf unnaturally allowed to live and consume grass intended for a sleeker elk herd? Did this imbalance cause several elk to starve to death later in the winter because the herd had outgrown its carrying capacity?

I'd like to say that the above anecdote was an isolated incident of human meddling, but I have scores of stories of unnatural interference with the perfect cycle of nature. And the end result is almost always a greater toll of life exacted later, far from the interloper's eyes.

Nature's Cure

In the natural world, the predator is not present to hurt, maim, and devour weaker animals in some macabre orgy of killing lust. Instead, nature has provided the predator to keep in check the rapidly multiplying rodent and bird populations.

So who controls the predators? The answer comes from two surprising sources—the prey animals themselves and other predators.

Life is hard for any predator, even during good times. It must literally run down and catch some of the fastest, most elusive prey animals in the world, with the difference between life and death often relying on the outcome of a single hunt.

For instance, if the fisher succeeds in catching a red squirrel, its body is nourished and retains its razor-sharp hunting instincts. If it fails on one hunt, it may lose a step chasing the next scampering squirrel. The result eventually is death, leaving only the strongest, fittest, luckiest predators to survive to hunt another day.

The pecking order among predators is no less lethal in a world where size means everything. Weighing only one-half pound, the ermine, which is the white winter phase of a weasel, is the smallest predator and is preyed upon by slightly larger predators such as the marten and fisher. But any marten or fisher that is not careful, in turn, gets preyed upon by a bobcat or lynx, which must be ever vigilant and stay close to the trees or the wolves and lions will tear them to pieces. And the wolf and lion must sleep with one eye open or the sudden rush of the mighty grizzly will change them from predator to prey in one powerful snap of its jaws.

Of course there are those who abhor all this killing and bemoan the violence afflicted upon the defenseless animals. They muse, "If only the killing would stop. Then the innocent animals could live happily ever after."

Not so! For nature has its own ways, though they are not our ways. From my many years of observing the ebb and flow and the triumph and tragedy in the natural world, I have come to one unshakable conclusion: All wild animals die a violent death.

Whether it is by claw or fang or the bitter storms of winter or disease or starvation, an animal's life is destined to end violently. Even if an elk can somehow escape the sudden charge of the grizzly bear or the lightening rush of the tawny lion, its fate remains a tragedy, for in the natural world there is no such thing as dying peacefully of old age.

With teeth worn down below the gums from years of grinding coarse vegetation, an older elk experiences much pain and suffering as it struggles to chew a few morsels of food. This is the paradox of the elk that lives to old age, that even with plentiful forage its demise is more prolonged and painful than the adrenalin-numbed death of the elk felled by the predator.

Anyone who doubts the destiny of the wild animal in nature should take a trip to Yellowstone National Park in early April after the long winter has finally relinquished its frigid grip upon the land. Hundreds of bison, elk, and deer stagger among healthy animals, eyes glazed, bodies wasted to hide-covered skeletons. Their condition may have been the result of an injury, old age, or being unlucky. Nevertheless, their starvation has been so complete that their bodies have turned cannibalistic and have begun to consume their own flesh, going so far as to even suck the very marrow from their bones.

For this well-fed human, it has been a traumatic learning experience to view the austere ways of nature. Watching a wild animal that I cherish slowly waste away over a period of weeks was often more than I could bear to watch. There were even a few times when I felt like grabbing a stout limb and putting a particular suffering animal out of its misery. In a perverse twist of emotions, I was actually relieved at first light when I found wolves feeding on a certain gaunt elk that I'd watched flounder in starvation-caused anguish for days. For me it was truly a turning point in my awkward journey toward becoming the natural man.

Grace

You don't have to forsake civilization and become a mountain man to understand the perfect cycle of nature. You just have to get to the point where a part of your heart and soul is in touch with its nuances.

You no longer step callously on the tiny scrambling ant. And yet, you can also celebrate the shedding of blood when it occurs naturally. You're finally free to ponder each entity's function and role in the wilderness through which you pass. The screeching hawk above, red-stained snow below—all begin to mesh into one living, breathing cycle of life that you feel more a part of with every stutter step to avoid squashing the struggling caterpillar.

And finally, the sight of a Yellowstone wolf carrying off a calf elk is understood and mentally balanced by the equally sober spectacle of another elk starving to death, thereby providing sustenance for other predators. After a while the sins of the killers are pardoned and ultimately understood as briefly violent but necessary parts of nature's perfect scheme.

This state of being has a name. It's called Grace.

THE CRITICAL PREY BASE

Snowshoe hare

Without prey animals, predators would disappear from the earth. And rightfully so, for in the cycle of nature the predator exists solely as a regulator of the plethora of nonlethal animals and birds.

Unable to live on a diet of grass or twigs like the mouse and the moose, a predator's metabolism demands flesh for nourishment. And while there is some degree of predation among the predators themselves, the greatest sustenance for the predator comes from the nonpredator species.

Generally, the prey base falls into three categories: rodents, birds, and large mammals. Some of the smaller predators, such as the ermine and marten, are forced by their size to rely on the smaller prey animals. Medium-sized predators, such as the bobcat and coyote, rely on both small and medium-sized prey for the majority of their sustenance but occasionally kill larger animals such as deer. On the other hand large predators such as wolves, mountain lions, and bears prey mostly on larger mammals in the ungulate family, such as deer, elk, and moose.

Rodents

The rodent family is capable of multiplying at an astounding rate and overrunning the world with a scurrying blanket of furry brown bodies. And it would, if not for the many predators who keep their numbers in check.

Conversely, these innocuous but loathsome creatures are literally the lifeblood of the predator. Every hunter, from the tiny ermine to the wolf, can usually count on catching a few juicy mice from a jumble of logs to stave off the dizzying effects of an empty belly.

It is difficult for the leisurely nature traveler to comprehend the magnitude of the rodent family because they are seldom seen, being mostly nocturnal and secretive, one result of their dubious status as favored prey. But when snow covers the ground, the telltale tracks of rodents can be seen bounding in every direction.

Tiny mouse tracks, larger pack-rat hoppings, along with a multitude of squirrel and rabbit tracks crisscross the snow. Their tracks show the haste with which these exposed prey animals scurry from one shelter to the next. Occasionally, a larger track coincides, leaving behind a disturbance in the snow—a few hairs and blood smear—as evidence of the predator/prey drama.

Mice

The common brown field mouse and the deer mouse resemble the same tiny rodent that occasionally takes up residence in our homes. Any log, overturned tree, or bush provides ample protection for a mouse. Consequently, they are found in great abundance literally everywhere in the wilderness and, not surprisingly, are staples of small and medium-sized predators. The slim weasels, such as the ermine and marten, often pursue a mouse right down through a tightly packed brush jumble; an ermine is tiny enough to often follow a mouse right down into its hole.

Mice also provide a large part of a medium-sized predator's diet. I've often watched coyotes sit motionless in a meadow, ears up, body erect and tense, as they prepare to pounce on a mouse. Suddenly, the coyote leaps high into the air and comes down with its four paws together to trap a mouse before the rodent can scurry away. So efficient are the coyote and bobcat at mousing that they can exist indefinitely on the half dozen mice they manage to catch daily.

However, a mouse weighs only about an ounce and is little more than an appetizer for a 120-pound wolf, which would literally starve to death expending the energy necessary to fill its belly with mice. The even larger mountain lion does not possess the nimbleness to catch a mouse and seldom seeks to hunt such small animals once it grows beyond the kitten stage. As a result most predators are always on the lookout for larger prey on which to expend their energy more efficiently.

Pack Rats

The prolific pack rat is found everywhere in the Rocky Mountains, ranging all the way from Mexico to northern Canada. It weighs about a half pound, furnishing a full meal for a coyote or bobcat. Unlike the ugly wharf rat of the city, the pack rat is an attractive (excuse the oxymoron) rodent with soft, dusty brown fur and large eyes. Its tail is long and furry, and it tends to move in great leaping bounds.

Pack rats inhabit rock crevices and log jumbles, where they often build elaborate nests of fur, pine needles, or grass. This is the same rodent that is famous for sneaking into cabins or camps and packing away coins, watches, rings, or anything else that is shiny and movable. These items are taken back to the nest and stored, for reasons known only to the pack rat.

Marten, ermine, fisher, coyote, and bobcat all hunt extensively for pack rats. I often detour from any planned route whenever I see a rock outcrop because these rock jumbles are favorite pack-rat haunts. Well-worn runs and droppings are telltale signs that a colony of pack rats lives there. In winter a profusion of pack-rat tracks can be seen in the snow as these cordial rodents hop around their home territory. Unfortunately for the pack rats, every passing predator also investigates these rock outcrops.

Red Squirrel

The red squirrel can be found in rural backyards alongside its cousins, the gray and fox squirrel. But the red squirrel's range extends far back into the wilderness, where it is the lone representative of the squirrel family.

The red squirrel prefers to dig its den in the ground at the base of a tree in dense coniferous forests where lots of pinecones grow. It cuts the cones from trees and stores them in several underground caches, eating the seeds through the lean winter months.

Within its half-acre home territory, a red squirrel will have one or two workshops. These are secure areas where the squirrel carries its food to eat. Workshops are easily recognizable by the 3-foot-high piles of discarded cone hulls, and they are the focal point of the squirrel's chief predator, the pine marten.

The red squirrel is quick as lightning and easily soars between trees. Unfortunately for the squirrel, the marten is a bit faster and can also soar right behind. Once a marten is in hot pursuit of a red squirrel, it's only a matter of time before it wins the race, unless the squirrel can reach its den. Even then, a smallish marten may squirm right down the den hole and still catch and kill the squirrel.

A few years ago, I'd taken two friends up to a remote backcountry lake that was teeming with native cutthroat trout. While we rested along the lakeshore after an arduous climb, a commotion in a spruce tree 20 feet away caught our attention.

Presently, a madly screaming red squirrel began a frantic spiraling descent down the tree trunk, with a pine marten in close pursuit. Both prey and predator hit the ground at the same time, and a furious commotion took place in the huckleberry brush. Suddenly, the red squirrel's hysterical scream was cut short.

Both men were very excited because it was the first marten they'd seen in the wild. I told them that we were very fortunate to have had a ringside seat to that incredible chase sequence.

The fisher, bobcat, coyote, and lynx also prey extensively on red squirrels. It's not surprising, then, that a red squirrel rarely lives longer than eighteen months. The red squirrel's population density and widespread distribution make it an important food source.

Snowshoe Hare

The snowshoe hare is a long-legged, lean rodent found in abundance throughout the forested and mountainous terrain of the Rockies, from Colorado north to Alaska, until the forest gives way to tundra. From there its cousin, the arctic hare, takes over.

The snowshoe is often referred to as the varying hare because its fur changes color, from dusty brown in summer to pure white in winter. This is due to a molting process of shedding its long white winter fur, leaving its brown summer undercoat, and then regrowing the long white winter coat.

Nature has wonderfully adapted the snowshoe hare for winter survival in its bitter cold, deep-snow environment. A white-furred hare sitting in the snow is virtually invisible, except for two tiny black ear tips and nose. Nature has also provided the snowshoe with oversize rear paws that allow it to glide over the top of deep, powdery snow, which often builds to 8 feet in depth, without floundering; hence, its name.

The snowshoe is an enormously important prey animal because, at three pounds, it represents a large source of protein. All wilderness predators except the slumbering grizzly bear and mountain lion depend to some degree on the snowshoe hare in winter. Fortunately, nature has provided this prolific rodent in high numbers throughout most of its range.

However, the snowshoe-hare population fluctuates in a perplexing boom-and-bust cycle that occurs roughly every seven years. For reasons unknown to scientists, snowshoe numbers remain constant for a few years, then begin to increase dramatically. Along with the explosion of hares comes a marked increase in the predators who hunt it. Though a host of predators gorge and gorge on the plentiful hares, they have no discernable impact on their rapid population rise.

Early naturalists in Canada's backwoods tell of snowshoe peaks when the woods literally crawled with hares. Everywhere eyes were cast, a snowshoe could be seen. It has been estimated that a population approaching 10,000 hares per square mile was not unusual during the peak of the cycle.

After building to such extraordinary numbers, disease sweeps through the hare population and wipes out the entire species, to the point where extinction seems apparent. But after a few years isolated hare sightings begin, until the creatures once more become plentiful, then overpopulated, and then crash again.

A traveler in central Manitoba related that he was walking along a railroad track during a peak snowshoe year. It was late fall, but snow had not yet arrived, though the hares had already grown their white winter coats. The traveler noted, "The place was eerie with all these white forms hopping over the bare ground everywhere I looked. The snowshoes were so numerous that they often did not even bother running away from me. I made a game of counting as many hares as I could from a standing position. Several times I counted more than fifty, and one time I counted seventy-six hares all within my sight."

The traveler returned the next spring and discovered the woods littered with thousands of snowshoe carcasses. Every few feet, another white body could be seen. For years after that great die-off, the man noted, no one saw a snowshoe hare.

Certain animals are true harbingers of wilderness, such as the fisher, the lynx, the wolf, and the grizzly. But so, too, is the snowshoe hare, for nature has provided this rodent in abundance to assure a prey base for those animals that steadfastly cling to the most remote corners of the world. But with the snowshoe's racehorse speed and agility, it's no free meal.

Beaver

A mature beaver weighs forty pounds or more, so this prolific rodent has the potential to provide a large source of food for both medium-sized and larger predators. In its flooded habitat a beaver is safe, but when it ventures into shallow water to build its dams, or onto land to cut down trees, the beaver is often preyed upon.

However, a big beaver is no pushover. I once watched a large beaver, ambushed while gnawing on a tree 30 feet from its pond, hold off two coyotes. Gnashing its wicked chisel teeth, the beaver repeatedly rushed the startled coyotes as it slowly edged toward the safety of the pond. With a furious lunge, the beaver splashed into deep water, leaving the startled coyotes to roam menacingly along the water's edge, occasionally tiptoeing a few feet into the pond, but lacking the courage to swim out and engage the beaver in its element.

This particular beaver seemed to enjoy swimming back and forth in deep water, tantalizingly close to the pacing, frustrated coyotes. Occasionally it would slap the water with its wide, flat, scaly tail—a universal signal for danger among beavers.

Medium-sized predators such as the coyote, bobcat, and lynx are capable of killing a beaver out of the water by sneaking up and pouncing on it while it is preoccupied. A quick bite to the back of the neck kills the beaver quickly.

Mountain lions and wolves have the size and power to easily kill the biggest beaver. I once followed a pack of six wolves for two days in northwest Montana, and the pack never trotted past a beaver dam without sending one member over to look for an easy meal.

Whenever I roam through the backcountry, I also take the time to search the muddy shoreline around beaver colonies for predator tracks.

The track most often found is the large pug mark of the mountain lion, which relishes the taste of beaver meat. One winter in the Great Burn Wilderness of western Montana, I located a huge beaver colony consisting of two main lodges and six ponds. I guessed this colony held about twelve beavers. The next time through, I found where a lion had stalked and killed a beaver that apparently was preoccupied gnawing at a small cottonwood tree 10 yards from the water's edge.

As the winter wore on and the beavers' food cache became depleted, the animals were forced to venture over to land to cut down trees. And the lion was waiting. Over a two-month period, I found seven lion kills. When I visited the ponds in spring there was no fresh beaver sign. My guess was the lion had wiped out the entire colony.

The beaver is an enormously important prey animal, not only because its large size furnishes a good supply of food for the larger predators, but also because the flooded habitat created by its dams draws in birds, which furnish added food potential.

Birds

Birds are seldom the main prey of a predator. They are too difficult to catch, and their airborne capability makes them too tentative to locate and hunt with any regularity. However, birds remain valuable prey for wilderness predators because they provide critical "fill-in" food.

The vast majority of wilderness birds—sparrows, chickadees, jays—weigh only a few ounces and provide little more than a mouthful to most predators, but that mouthful often makes the difference between life and death.

A frustrated pine marten that has failed on several red-squirrel hunts over three days may crawl into a brushy thicket, exhausted and famished. Shortly a chickadee flitters through the brush, busily pecking at berries, and hops within a few feet of the motionless marten. In a blur the sparrow is seized and quickly devoured. The tiny sparrow is enough to fill the marten's belly and nourish it for another hunt.

Larger birds, such as grouse and ducks, weigh about two pounds and can sustain a medium-sized predator for a few days. Forest-dwelling grouse species—the ruffed, spruce, and the Franklin's—are abundant, and telegraph their presence to predators by drumming or cooing in early spring during mating rituals; in summer the flightless newborn chicks are easy pickings. Farther north, the ptarmigan is an abundant prey bird and valuable food source for all predators.

Waterfowl are extremely wary, but in deep winter and spring predators find good hunting along narrow waterways for bank-hugging ducks. Canada and snow geese, ranging in weight from six to ten pounds, provide a substantial meal for even the largest predator. These birds avoid swimming or landing close to brush or logs, where a predator may be hiding. Unfortunately, this is not always possible, and some of these birds are killed when they venture close to shore.

One day in British Columbia, I was watching a mother goose and six half-grown goslings paddle along an 8-foot-wide stream channel that connected the Athabasca River to a slough. No sooner had it entered my mind that the channel was a dangerous place when a coyote charged out of the high grass along the bank and dove into the midst of the geese. Amidst a cacophony of hysterical honking and flying water, I lost sight of the coyote. But when the flustered mother goose entered the river channel, she was followed by only five goslings.

While the rodent family comprises the bulk of the prey base, birds are valuable as alternative prey for every size predator. While traveling between prime snowshoe-hare haunts, the lynx often supplements its diet with an occasional ptarmigan or grouse. And when the wolf or mountain lion investigates the beaver pond, these predators also scan the water's edge for any unsuspecting geese or ducks.

Large Mammals

Large mammals—deer, goats, sheep, elk, and moose—are the main prey of the larger predators such as the wolf, mountain lion, and black and grizzly bears. These large predators are not picky about which species they hunt. Along the North Fork Flathead River near Glacier National Park, deer are plentiful, so the wolf pack's diet consists of 94 percent whitetail deer. In Yellowstone National Park, where elk are abundant, wolves rely almost totally on this species.

Medium-sized predators, such as the coyote, bobcat, lynx, and wolverine normally cannot bring down a creature the size of a deer. However, a sick or injured deer is fair prey for these animals. Also, deep snow that slows down a deer often induces these predators to pursue it, and kills result.

Turning the Tables

Paradoxically, a prey animal the size of a tiny mouse has the potential to turn the tables on its adversary and actually bring about its demise. You can best understand this phenomenon by watching your house cat play with a mouse (or a toy). It grabs the mouse and throws it into the air. To the casual observer, the cat is playing with the mouse. That's true to some degree, but the main purpose of the cat's action, done instinctively, is to quickly bite the mouse and then get rid of it before the diminutive rodent sinks its sharp, chiseled teeth into the soft flesh of the cat's mouth.

That is exactly the method that small prey animals use to wreak vengeance, albeit post-mortem, on a predator. A coyote that pounces on a rat runs the risk of receiving a nasty bite if the rodent is not immediately disabled and released.

Oftentimes a rodent bite amounts to little more than a scratch. But within days infection sets in, and with it the possibility of blood poisoning. But even if a predator doesn't die directly from the bite, the infected wound may slow it enough to keep it from catching prey, and death from starvation results.

I've observed many predators with noticeable limps that, upon closer scrutiny, proved to be a swollen paw that I guessed was the result of a thorn or sharp rock. But after watching several predator/prey encounters go awry, my guess now is that many unknown infirmities among predators result from infected prey bites.

A classic example of a small prey animal turning the tables on a predator occurred a few years ago near the Selway-Bitterroot Wilderness Area in Idaho, where I sat under a ponderosa pine watching a frozen muskrat slough. The muskrats were forced to leave their ice-bound home and travel 50 feet to a small stream with open water. As I watched a large muskrat waddle across the ice, a smallish bobcat streaked out of the trees, but the slippery ice caused it to slide right past the muskrat.

The muskrat dove for the bank, but couldn't find an escape hole, so the two-pound rodent backed against the bank and bared its yellow rat teeth at the young bobcat, which had recovered from its unscheduled slippery detour and quickly closed in on the animal. When the bobcat lunged, the rodent latched onto its upper lip. The startled cat jumped 3 feet into the air with the muskrat still hanging on.

When predator and prey crashed back to the ice, the muskrat released its grip and scurried along the bank and into a hole. The bobcat pawed at its face and shook its head several times before padding over to the hole and sniffing around before wandering off—without dinner and with a potentially fatal wound.

Large prey animals such as deer, elk, and moose also have the potential to deliver a powerful wallop with their sharp hooves, and even the grizzly bear must be careful when attacking an animal the size of a moose. That's why predators such as the lion rely on stealth and surprise to take down large prey before it can deliver a kick.

And sometimes, the prey actually wins. A few years ago a large female wolf was found dead in Idaho's Boise National Forest. Suspecting foul play, wildlife biologists autopsied the carcass and discovered that the wolf had died from massive head trauma consistent with a kick from an elk. But even if a predator is not killed outright, a few broken ribs or an injured shoulder is often enough to slow down a large predator and doom it to starvation, though at times a predator may find enough food, such as winter-killed deer or elk, to sustain it while a nagging injury heals.

Wolves are especially careful to avoid taking chances while hunting. Seldom will a pack run down and kill a moose. Instead, the wolves circle and harass the animal, occasionally darting forward and tearing away a fist-sized chunk of flesh before jumping back, until the moose grows weak from shock, exhaustion, and blood loss. This torture may last for upwards of a day and remains a traumatic spectacle for a human to behold.

But even when the pack moves in to finish off a weakened animal, it is not unusual for a wolf to be injured during the final fray. This injured animal, by exhibiting its weakness, is then shunned by the pack and often left behind or banned from feeding on a kill when it finally catches up to the healthy pack. Wolf packs have even killed a lame pack member that hung around after being shunned.

In my opinion prey animals are as fascinating to observe as the predators who hunt them. Whenever I sit quietly and watch a wary snowshoe hare float across deep snow, I think of the lynx that will surely come searching some ghostly night. A red squirrel scolding me as I walk by brings visions of a frantic chase with a pine marten in close pursuit, and when a tiny mouse scurries for cover, I expect an ermine to dart forward.

The intricacies of nature become most apparent when one studies the phenomenal variety and abundance of prey animals and birds that sustain predators. And it leaves us with a delicious rhetorical question: Is the prey created to sustain the predator, or is the predator created to sustain the prey?

THE GRIZZLY BEAR

Grizzly country is a pristine land of lush alpine meadows resplendent with velvety carpets of wildflowers and snow-capped mountains rising to the heavens, and soaring eagles, and goats and sheep, and bull elk and moose. True, there are other places of equal beauty, but the presence of the great bear transforms this land into a place of awe and legend.

It's also a place of raw emotion and primal instinct. From the moment you start up the trail in grizzly country, you sense the roles are reversed. You're no longer at the top of the food chain, for on this hallowed ground roams a lumbering quarter ton of taut muscle and silver-tipped fur that is exponentially bigger, stronger, faster than any human. You tread lightly, your movements become furtive. Your senses are acute, eyes probing every shadow, ears straining to detect the sound of danger, even your nose monitoring the air currents for the sickly sweet odor of death—an indication that a grizzly may be guarding a kill nearby.

In this place you are a guest. It would be rude and dangerous to behave otherwise. For without proclamation you are compelled to conform to a different standard, one without Miranda rights or due process, without a legal system that protects the young and the innocent, or the old and the innocent. And while this place lacks premeditated malice, it is also a place where might is always right, and survival is awarded to the swift, the strong, the cunning—and the lucky.

But for those brave enough and open-minded enough to accept these new rules and challenges, grizzly country becomes truly a holy place to visit and commune with the great bear. You come to crave it like a wilderness narcotic, adrenalin rushing through your veins while an ominous sense of impending confrontation keeps your breath ragged and clipped. You feel more alive than you've ever felt before; you notice things, feel things, sense things, appreciate things that were formerly dismissed as mundane.

In our modern age of human apathy and lethargy, to experience such a quickening of the body, mind, and spirit reminds us why Native Americans called the grizzly "Spirit Bear" and formed bear societies in an effort to somehow forge a spiritual kinship. Conversely, the grizzly in no way reciprocates such feelings of human camaraderie, then or now, and remains a solitary animal the primary urges of which are simply to eat, sleep, mate, and be left alone.

Grizzlies Are Always Hungry

A bear's stomach governs most of its activity because of the stress of hibernation, that period of slumber during the five months of winter when deep snow and arctic cold blanket the wilderness. The grizzly is both half-starved and ravenously pursuing anything of food value after it emerges from hibernation in early spring, or it is on a manic quest for food in late summer to add an ample layer of fat before the snows of fall once more bury the land.

The grizzly is an omnivore, meaning it eats both vegetation and flesh. In the spring, when the bear groggily emerges from its den, it hungrily devours succulent shoots of grass and chomps on a variety of forbes, such as wild parsnips and glacier lilies. To help the grizzly put on fat before hibernation, nature provides the low-bush huckleberry, which grows on open slopes in the high country. In late summer the grizzly roams extensively in search of this high-sugar fruit. When a bear locates a berry patch, it strips berries, leaves, and stems and quickly puts on weight. So important is the huckleberry to the great bear's existence that the grizzlies in Glacier National Park travel 20 miles or more to get to the berry patches high up on Huckleberry Mountain along the western border of the park. In early September I've counted upwards of eight grizzlies feeding on berries here. Sadly, all these berry patches burned during the wildfire season of 2003, when well-meaning but ignorant firefighters purposely burned these areas, setting backfires to protect a few homes near the hamlet of West Glacier. It will take twenty years for these berry patches to grow back, and it remains to be seen what impact the loss of this critical food source has on these grizzlies.

Watching a portly grizzly graze on grass, or amiably nip at huckleberries, it's hard to visualize it as a supreme predator. But don't be misled. The grizzly is always on the lookout for protein in the form of meat, such as the rancid carcass of a winter-killed elk, or a bighorn sheep swept to its death from an avalanche. Nor is the grizzly adverse to creating its own carrion; when opportunity arises, it can change in an instant from a benign grazer into a cunning predator.

A Cunning Predator

A few years ago, I was scouting for grizzlies in the Many Glacier area on the eastern slopes of Glacier National Park. It was late April and the bears had emerged from hibernation, but the spring grass had not yet pushed up. I was watching a herd of eight mountain goats 400 yards away, bedded on a rocky ridge above a protected bowl that had begun greening up. A large boar, or male, grizzly ambled into sight and, ignoring the goats in the rocks above, began feeding on a small patch of sedges, which resemble small shrublike plants. The bear fed across the bowl while the goats watched tensely from about 150 yards away. When the grizzly fed out of sight, the goats relaxed and went back to lazing in the spring sun and chewing their cuds.

Out of sight of the goats, the grizzly's disposition changed immediately. The bear hurried to the base of the rock cliff and began climbing the steep terraces in a route that would take him around and above the goats. I lost sight of the grizzly when he entered a narrow crevice, and I guessed that he had continued upward and over the ridge. I went back to glassing the goats, but a minute later the herd suddenly scattered as the grizzly thundered into their midst at a full gallop. The goats scrambled down the rock face, easily escaping the bear.

To the casual observer, the grizzly was foolish to have expended so much energy in a fruitless charge at the goats, animals adept at maneuvering along the sheer rock walls. But I knew better. The leading cause of death among goats is an accidental fall. That boar grizzly was not trying to catch a goat, he was trying to "create" an accident.

Another time, I watched a grizzly roaming the rocky ridges above Elizabeth Lake in the Many Glacier area and chasing every herd of goats and bighorn sheep it encountered. I didn't see the bear catch a ewe (female) bighorn, but the next day when I spotted the bear, it was feeding on a bighorn sheep carcass.

The "amiably feeding bear" ploy is a favorite hunting method of the grizzly that works well on other prey besides goats and sheep. Several years ago I was filming grizzlies in Yellowstone for a documentary. It was a balmy late June evening, and I was watching a dozen cow elk with their calves in a meadow along the foothills of Dunraven Pass. Suddenly the cows grew alert; all their eyes were on a small grove of lodgepole pine trees 300 yards away.

A medium-sized brown grizzly emerged from the trees. At that distance, the fleet-footed elk could have easily outdistanced the bear. But instead of giving chase, the bear began munching on grass, seemingly ignoring the elk. The bear fed away from the elk and they relaxed, then stiffened when the predator began feeding toward them. Again the bear turned away. This went on for close to an hour, and I could see that the cows, though still wary, had grown less cautious, even though the bear's meanderings had brought him to about 150 yards of the elk.

The bear turned away from the elk for a few seconds, and then suddenly charged the herd. The startled cows fled in every direction. The grizzly galloped after one cow and her calf, but the elk easily stayed ahead of the bear. This mismatch continued for several hundred yards, but then the bear began to gain ground as the calf tired. In a marshy area, the bear put on a burst of speed and caught the calf. The frantic mother came back to help, and narrowly escaped a vicious swipe by the grizzly. The bear then proceeded to tear the calf apart. This dramatic film sequence, along with a good example of a bear chasing goats to "create an accident," can be seen in the video "Bear Attacks."

Big Grizzlies Kill Smaller Grizzlies

Grizzlies are no less lethal among themselves. One of the leading causes of death among smaller grizzlies is an attack by a boar. A mature male jealously protects his home territory and will not tolerate another male in his area, which may extend several square miles. Younger male bears must stake out their own home range, or they will be killed and eaten by the dominant male in an area. This antagonistic behavior by a boar grizzly also extends to cubs, with the big male attacking a cub for the sole purpose of preying on it for food. The only thing that keeps him from pouncing on every cub he encounters is the fierce fight put up by the protective sow, or female, grizzly. Only the biggest, most aggressive boars attempt such a hazardous move.

A wilderness traveler in Canada related how he sat on a bluff and watched a large boar grizzly stalk two cubs playing along a stream while the sow dug for grubs a short distance away. The boar pounced on one of the cubs and began shaking it. The sow responded to her cub's squealing with a bellow of rage and, with teeth snapping, came to her cub's rescue. The boar, more than twice the sow's size, dropped the cub and pummeled the sow's face with its long, daggerlike claws. The sow staggered backwards, her face a mass of blood and torn flesh, but she came forward once again when the boar bit into her screaming cub. This time the boar sent several sledgehammer blows into the sow's face and bit her in the throat and shook her. While the sow lay gasping her last breaths, the boar returned to the cub and proceeded to tear it apart and eat it. The male then chased down the other cub and killed it. Small wonder, then, that early naturalists such as Lewis and Clark, named this bear *Ursus horribilis,* meaning Terrible Bear.

I encountered a sow in Yellowstone National Park in June of 2002 that may have survived a similar experience. One morning I was hiking along the spine of a rocky ridge, hoping to photograph a grizzly bear in the meadow below. A large sow loped from the timber about 300 yards away, with two cubs hurrying behind her. Through my binoculars I saw that the sow's lower jaw was misshapen, jutting out in a pronounced overbite that exposed both of her lower canines. Her head was also cocked to the left. These facial injuries, I guessed, came from an altercation with a boar.

Another thing that impressed me about this particular sow was her constant hysterical disposition. Whenever she stopped, she whirled one way, then another, nervously pacing and sniffing the air for danger. My guess was that she had lost her cubs to a large boar in the past, and she didn't intend to have that happen again.

I saw this sow six different times over the next three days as she hunted through the sagebrush fringes, which are favorite places for cow elk to hide their calves. And every time the sow was at a nervous lope or was flat-out running. I felt sorry for her cubs because they were hard-pressed to keep up with her.

Grizzlies Avoid Man—to a Point

The only creature capable of making even the mighty grizzly wary is man. Though no one knows for sure why a creature as mighty as the grizzly would run away from a physically inferior human, my opinion is that through the millennia, the grizzly learned the hard way that the frail-looking *Homo sapiens* were every bit as cunning and deadly, with their sharp sticks and pits and traps and guns.

When I asked Chuck Jonkel, one of the foremost grizzly experts in the world, why a grizzly would avoid a human, he chuckled and replied, "Because they've learned that being around man gets them killed." Call it instinct, or hard lessons learned through the ages, but the grizzly avoids man. It's also my guess that the grizzly seeks wilderness, in part, to escape the emotional and physical trappings of civilization, from the yapping of dogs to the labyrinth of roads in the lower country that carry the startling roars of cars and trucks.

But neither is the grizzly a coward. Primal instincts deep within the genetic code of the grizzly bear prompt it to react aggressively when surprised or confronted, no doubt harkening back to the Pleistocene Epoch, when the grizzly first appeared. It was an age when other large predators, such as the giant brown bear and saber-toothed tiger, also roamed the land. A chance encounter with one of these equally lethal predators put the grizzly's existence in peril, with escape by fleeing not always successful. To survive such an encounter, the grizzly developed an aggressive-defensive posture of rushing forward when startled and neutralizing its attacker before fleeing.

This is exactly how most grizzly attacks unfold, with a hiker, or fisherman, or hunter stumbling upon a bear at close range. Though bellowing with rage, the animal actually feels threatened by this sudden penetration of its safe zone. It has no way of knowing, for instance, that the intruder is just a 105-pound grandmother with nothing but love in her heart for the bear. The frightened grizzly rushes forward and swats the intruder, or bites and shakes it, before fleeing. A grizzly can inflict horrible injuries to the human body with a single bite, or a swat from its massive paw and 4-inch-long claws.

South Dakota resident Sonja Crowley was on a guided elk-hunting trip 20 miles north of Yellowstone National Park with her husband, Morey, when fate, in the form of a warm spell, put her on a collision course with an enraged sow grizzly. Morey had killed a bull elk the day before in a high basin and told his wife that there were several other bulls still up there. The next morning Sonja and her guide, Joe Heimer, started the long climb to the basin an hour before daybreak.

By November grizzlies are normally in their dens snoring away the winter, but a warm spell had descended upon the area, turning the snow to mush and reawakening the bears. Sonja and Joe had already yanked off their winter coats before dawn, and Joe offered to carry Sonja's rifle to ease her burden.

They eased to the top of a ridge and were scouring the hills for elk when Sonja tapped Joe on the shoulder and pointed to their left. A sow grizzly with three cubs was pawing through the snow 200 feet away. Hunter and guide slowly backed away and stepped behind a juniper bush. At that point, the sow and cubs were at ease. Then the wind shifted. When their scent reached the sow, she immediately charged them.

Joe yelled, hoping to turn the sow, but when she kept coming he snapped the rifle to his shoulder. Still, he hesitated. The grizzly was a protected species. And besides, he liked the bears. He waited until the last second to shoot. He waited too long. With the enraged sow just a few feet away and coming fast, he pointed the barrel of the gun at her head and fired, but missed.

The sow knocked Joe flat, sending the rifle flying. The bear bit deep into his right knee, until he kicked her in the face with his left leg, whereupon the bear bit that leg and shook him fiercely.

Joe was yelling for help, and Sonja bravely came to his aid by going for the rifle. The bear saw the movement and went after her. Sonja started to run, but the sow knocked her down and bit her head and shook her like a rag doll. As suddenly as the attack began, it ended when the bear dropped Sonja and ran back to her cubs. Joe limped over to Sonja lying in the snow and he gasped. The left side of her face was gone, hanging by a flap of skin that exposed teeth and a broken jawbone.

Joe heard the sow huffing behind him and turned to see her coming at him again. This time he was ready and put a slug from the 7mm magnum rifle into her shoulder. The bear dropped, and Joe hastily returned to helping Sonja. He carefully laid her face in place, but she looked behind him and emitted a gurgling scream. The bear was hobbling at him, just a few feet away. Joe raised the rifle and sent a bullet into her brain. The bear slid to a halt literally between his legs.

When I interviewed Joe a few years later, he was still haunted by contrasting emotions—for taking the life of the sow grizzly and for not killing her sooner because of the injuries to Sonja. Amazingly, surgeons were able to reconstruct Sonja Crowley's face, but she lost most of the sight in one eye and carries six steel plates in her head, reminders of the dangers of surprising a grizzly at close range.

Most of the time there is an uneasy truce between man and bear. Humans keep their distance and the great bear ignores them. But occasionally, well-meaning people, some of them even bear lovers, invade the grizzly's domain and consciously break the rules to prove to the public, and maybe even to the bear, that humans and bears can live in harmony together. Such irresponsible actions are a death sentence in grizzly country.

Timothy Treadwell was such a man. Treadwell entered the limelight and turned heads by publicly disagreeing with bear specialists who adamantly espouse a doctrine of avoidance. Treadwell appeared on the Discovery Channel, David Letterman, and the "Rosie O'Donnell Show" to talk about "his" bears, giving them names such as Boobie, Aunt Melissa, Mr. Chocolate, and Freckles. On the "Tom Snyder Show," Treadwell told interviewer Snyder that the bears allowed him to move in close because he was no threat to their food sources, and that he further allayed their instinctive intolerance of humans by intoning soothing words of love. Treadwell then showed a film clip of large coastal grizzlies passing within feet of him along an Alaska stream while he crooned the words, "I love you. I love you."

What was not explained about the film segment was that Treadwell was dealing with a very small segment of grizzlies in Katmai National Park, where the animals gorge themselves on spawning salmon. In fact the U.S. Park Service had even installed bear observation platforms along these streams so bear lovers could watch from close range while the animals captured and fed upon on the fish.

Treadwell continued making forays to Katmai to film himself, often moving so close to feeding bears that he could almost touch them. In the meantime Treadwell's notoriety among bear lovers grew, prompting the "National Geographic Explorer" television program to film his exploits at Katmai. Bear experts just shook their heads. They understood Treadwell was committing the cardinal sin in bear country, purposely moving in close to a bear.

On the afternoon of October 5, 2003, the price for breaking the rules in grizzly country came due for Timothy Treadwell and his companion, Amie Huguenard. When a bush pilot arrived the next morning to pick them up, he found their camp trashed and a large grizzly feeding on what looked like a human carcass. Authorities were notified, and later that day two rangers were flown in to investigate. They landed close to the camp and had advanced only a short distance when a large grizzly charged them and they killed it. They discovered the bear had been guarding his food cache. When they removed the covering of sticks and dirt from the cache, they discovered the partially eaten remains of Treadwell and Huguenard. As the rangers sifted through the ruined camp, another smaller bear appeared and showed aggressive tendencies, so it was killed also.

Investigators are normally at a loss to piece together the circumstances leading up to such a tragedy, but in this case they found a valuable piece of evidence: Treadwell's video camera. When they played the film back, it revealed several scenes of Treadwell moving in close, sometimes within mere feet, of several bears. Then the picture went black, but the sound continued, sending chills up their spines.

The five-minute audio segment began with Treadwell encountering a bear outside the tent, and Amie inside, probably turning on the camera. Treadwell suddenly began to yell for help as he was attacked by a bear. Amie could be heard screaming hysterically, "Play dead, Timothy! Don't fight it!" Treadwell, screaming amidst the roars of the bear, was heard pleading, "Hit it over the head with the frying pan!" Investigator Chris Hill was quoted as saying, "There's so much noise going on, I don't know what's him and what might be an animal. I keep hearing it in my mind. It's pretty disturbing."

The investigation officially concluded that by setting up his camp very close to a major bear trail, Treadwell had violated the first commandment of proper behavior in bear country: Always observe bears from a distance and avoid any action that stress or confront a bear.

Timothy Treadwell was not a bad person. He truly loved bears. His intention was to show the world that these animals were not dangerous and that man, by showing love and respect, could indeed form a bond of trust with the bears. As a result he and his companion were killed, along with two bears. His epitaph will read that his well-meaning but mis-guided actions produced the exact opposite effect on the public, as a fresh wave of hysteria toward the grizzly bear rippled through the country in the aftermath of his death.

Proper Behavior in Bear Country

The grizzly bear need not be feared, but it should be respected. The great bear is not out to maim and kill every human it encounters. On the con-trary it just wants to be left alone as it goes about its life. The vast major-ity of recreationists in bear country seldom have a problem when they behave properly.

Essentially, there are three situations with a grizzly that should be avoided: startling a bear; disturbing a bear guarding its food; and getting near a sow with cubs.

Grizzlies don't react well to surprises. Ninety percent of bear attacks occur when a human moves within 60 yards before the grizzly becomes aware of his or her presence, triggering the bear's aggressive-defensive reaction. The best way to avoid this very dangerous situation is to consciously determine to stay away from any bear you see. You can still enjoy the thrill of watching a grizzly, even from long range, by using binoculars. When hiking along a brushy trail where sight distance is limited, make lots of noise by yelling or singing to let the bear know you're coming, giving it plenty of time to retreat without feeling threatened.

A grizzly bear is a glutton, and when it finds or kills a large animal, it will jealously guard and defend the food source. Several people in recent years have been mauled, and a few killed, when they stumbled upon a carcass. The best way to avoid this extremely dangerous situation is to watch out for concentrations of ravens or crows because these birds flock to carrion. Also, if you smell something rotten, back away from that area, because if you can smell it, chances are great that any bears in the area will also have smelled it. And if you see a fresh mound of scraped-up dirt and twigs, it's probably a bear's food cache, covered to keep birds and other scavengers off the carcass. Quietly retreat and go back the way you came.

It should be no surprise that most attacks are attributed to female grizzlies. A sow will fiercely protect her cubs from danger, be it real, in the form of a predatory boar, or perceived, in the form of a hiker walking a forest trail. Never move toward a sow with cubs, even when the bears are far away, because a sow may still feel threatened. I know of three people who were attacked by a sow grizzly even though they were more than 100 yards away. If you see a sow with cubs, quietly retreat and make a wide circle of that area, or hike in a different direction.

You may be a careful traveler who obeys all the rules of proper behavior in bear country, but sometimes even that's not enough. Through no fault of your own, you may still come face to face with a grizzly bear at close range. When that happens, it is vital to be prepared in such a way that allows you, and the bear, to part ways unharmed.

Montana bowhunter Mark Matheny learned that lesson the hard way. Mark was in a good mood as he hiked down a ridge trail in the mountains north of Yellowstone National Park with his hunting partner, Fred

Bohnson. They were headed back to the trailhead at a brisk pace to bring back a horse after Mark had killed a mule deer buck earlier in the day. Mark was leading the way when several squawking crows flew up about 30 yards to his left. He looked over just in time to see a large brown grizzly bound over a log and come at him with two half-grown cubs trailing. Mark threw up his bow to fend off the charging bear, but she swatted it out of his hands and slammed him to the ground, then bit his face and head and shook him violently. Fred Bohnson advanced with a small can of pepper spray, but the bear swatted it out of his hands, knocked him down and bit him on the back and shoulder before returning to again savage Mark. Fred, though hurt and bleeding, retrieved the pepper spray, and when the sow turned toward him once more he sprayed her in the face. The sow bellowed, pawed at her face, and galloped into the forest with her cubs scrambling to keep up.

Though hurt and bleeding, Mark was able to hobble back to the trailhead with Fred's help. His wounds healed, but not his resolve to furnish the public with the best bear pepper spray possible. Mark founded UDAP (Universal Defense Alternative Products) and markets bear pepper spray in twelve- and fifteen-ounce cans licensed by the Environmental Protection Agency (EPA). Only EPA-approved sprays may be sold as bear pepper spray.

I've sprayed two bears and one mountain lion with UDAP bear pepper spray, and I can attest to its effectiveness. I've also interviewed dozens of men and women who stopped charging grizzly and black bears with bear pepper spray. If you venture into bear country, always carry pepper spray, because you never know when the unforeseen, the unexpected, or the unthinkable may occur. Just think how differently it would have ended for Timothy Treadwell and Amie Huguenard if they had been carrying bear pepper spray.

Species Description

Was that bear you saw a grizzly or a black bear? It seems like a simple question because black bears are black, right? Wrong! It's not enough to identify a bear by color alone. Black bears in the Rockies are often brown, even blond, in color. Conversely, some grizzlies are dark brown and even black. This blending of color variations between black and grizzly bears results in a handful of mistaken grizzly deaths each year when the great bear is mistaken for a black bear during spring black-bear hunting season.

The grizzly is protected and cannot be hunted in Montana. As a result, the Montana Department of Fish, Wildlife & Parks now requires any first-time black-bear hunter to pass a bear identification test before he or she can be issued a license.

The surest way to identify a grizzly is by its shoulder hump. Black bears have rounded shoulders that do not extend above the back, while a grizzly will have a pronounced shoulder hump. A grizzly's face is also more rounded and dished, with a somewhat pinched nose, while a black bear's head is sloped and its muzzle more pointed. Also, a grizzly's claws are between 4 and 5 inches long and their ivory color shows well, while a black bear's claws are usually less than 2 inches long.

Habitat

When Lewis and Clark visited the West, the grizzly was numerous and inhabited most of the countryside, from river bottoms to forested and mountainous terrain and the open prairies. As civilization encroached on grizzly habitat in the plains and lower lands, the grizzly was exterminated from these areas. Only those bears that preferred the more remote Rocky Mountain backcountry survived.

Unlike other predators such as the black bear, which can flourish in a variety of environments—even the low country along the edge of civilization—the grizzly's habitat requirements are much more restrictive. The great bear requires unroaded and uninhabited high-country wilderness, due mainly to its solitary nature, and its aversion to sharing its home range with man.

John and Frank Craighead pioneered satellite telemetry in the 1980s to identify prime grizzly habitat in the Rockies, and their work has become invaluable for biologists who work today to reintroduce grizzlies into some of their former range. The Craigheads found that grizzlies prefer a distinctive band of forested lands just below timberline, where their food sources, such as summering elk and deer and succulent plants, are most plentiful. In Glacier National Park most grizzlies are spotted feeding on plants in avalanche chutes grown over with vegetation, or roaming along the edges of alpine meadows. In Yellowstone grizzlies are most often seen roaming the valley bottoms where the grass and plants are still succulent, and big game animals are in abundance.

Range and Population

Due to loss of critical habitat and poor bear management practices by state and federal wildlife agencies, the grizzly was on the verge of extinction in the lower forty-eight states just four decades ago. When its population dipped below 200 in Yellowstone and Glacier and the states of Montana, Wyoming, and Idaho, the great bear was placed on the Endangered Species List as "threatened." This designation led to a slow turnaround, as dedicated wildlife biologists worked to protect remaining bear habitat. Today the grizzly population is climbing toward 2,000; Yellowstone National Park has about 400 bears, while Glacier counts about 500. In addition, some 400 grizzlies inhabit Montana lands outside the national park boundaries. Idaho has about 100 bears in the mountains west of Yellowstone. In Wyoming the grizzly bear is rapidly expanding south of Yellowstone National Park into areas of prime habitat, and bear numbers are pushing 400. Wyoming's neighboring states—Utah and Colorado—may harbor grizzlies in the future as the bears disperse throughout Wyoming. A remnant population of grizzlies may still exist in southern Colorado's remote South San Juan Mountain Range, as evidenced by sightings, scat, and bear diggings. A small population of twelve grizzlies now resides in the Northern Cascade and Selkirk Mountains of northern Washington.

North of the border, Canada's grizzly bear numbers remain healthy, with estimates ranging upwards of 30,000 bears roaming the vast wilderness areas of the Rockies. Alaska's bear population is sizable and stable at about 40,000 grizzlies.

Mating

Male and female grizzlies avoid each other except during mating season. A female is usually four years old before she comes into estrus sometime in mid-June. An investigating male will sniff the female's pheromones and become excited, whereupon he will court the female by rubbing against her and play-fighting. This is uncharacteristic behavior of a boar grizzly and occurs only during the mating period. But the boar's docile nature changes to rage when he sees another male approaching; vicious fights between competing males are not uncommon during mating season. When the female is receptive, the male mates her, often copulating for twenty minutes or more, and will stay with the female for several days and mate her numerous times. But as soon as she is out of estrus, the male wanders off in search of another receptive female.

While hibernating, a sow grizzly gives birth to between two and four cubs, though two is the norm. Hairless and blind at birth and weighing only about two pounds, the cubs grow quickly, nourished by the sow's milk, which is four times richer than cow's milk. By the time the female leaves her den in spring, the fully furred cubs weigh about twenty pounds and can easily follow their mother. The cubs stay with the sow for two years and are weaned from her when she comes into estrus the next spring. At this time the sow will rough up the yearling cubs, which usually weigh 150–200 pounds, and drive them away, or a mature male will run them off when he approaches the female to mate her.

THE BLACK BEAR

few years ago I photographed a 150-pound bear on Landowner Mountain in Glacier National Park in late August while it was chomping on huckleberries. This bear had a charcoal-colored coat and round face characteristic of a grizzly. Though it lacked the tell-tale humped shoulders of a grizzly, this is often the case with subadults, and I was certain it was a young grizzly. I later showed a photo of this bear to two bear biologists, who agreed with me that it was a grizzly, while others disagreed. Fortunately, this bear had an orange tag in its ear. By using a magnifying glass on the photograph taken of the bear, I was able to read the tag number (405) and sent a letter to park officials requesting species clarification. It came back: black bear.

That's how difficult it can be to identify a Rocky Mountain black bear, especially in grizzly country. Not surprisingly, most of the grizzly sightings I've investigated that proved false were actually brown-colored black bears that people assumed were grizzlies. That's because Rocky Mountain black bears, unlike their Midwestern namesakes, aren't always black, but come in color phases ranging from red, to blond, to brown—as in grizzly brown. Sadly, black-bear hunters in Montana accidentally shoot a handful of grizzly bears every year when they mistake them for brown-colored black bears. (Montana now requires black-bear hunters to pass a visual test to avoid accidental grizzly killings.)

Black Bears Are Adaptable

Unlike the grizzly, which requires very specific remote wilderness habitat, the black bear is highly adaptable and can be found in a variety of terrains, from the dense coniferous forests of the northern Rockies to the treeless alpine habitat at 14,000 feet in the central Rockies of Colorado and the arid cactus and juniper forests in the southern Rockies.

This adaptability heavily influences each species' population dynamics. While the grizzly struggles to maintain its presence in many of its historic haunts due to the encroachment of civilization, black bear numbers are stable or even growing. Statistics from 2003 show the grizzly population throughout the Rockies numbered at about 1,000, while black bear numbers topped 120,000. Black-bear numbers in Canada's Rocky Mountain provinces approach a quarter million, and Alaska's best estimate is about 50,000 black bears.

Black Bears Avoid Confrontation

The greatest difference between a grizzly and black bear lies in their temperament, which can best be described by this hypothetical encounter: A 200-pound black bear meets a 200-pound grizzly on a forest trail. The tendency of the black bear is to flee, while the grizzly's tendency is to run down the black bear, then kill and eat it.

This stark contrast in personality—aggression for the grizzly, avoidance for the black bear—defines each species. A black bear would rather flee than fight. And why not? It is not tied to a very narrow type of habitat that must be protected and defended to the death, as with the grizzly. Nor is the black bear generally as big (most mature black bears weigh 300 pounds or less) or as powerful as the grizzly. So why fight and risk injury or death?

Sometimes running away isn't enough. A grizzly bear can often overtake a black bear in a foot race. That's why the black bear's primary safety is found in the trees. Its 1½-inch-long claws sink into the bark, allowing a black bear to effortlessly scale any tree, limbs or not. Grizzlies can also climb trees, though they are not as nimble as their smaller cousin. The grizzly is not able to sink its 4-inch-long claws into tree bark—instead, it must hook its paws over each limb and pull itself up.

I once watched a black bear/grizzly confrontation south of Yakutat, Alaska. I was hiking along an old logging road when I spotted a 300-pound sow black bear with two small cubs. The bears were pawing at a rotten log, lapping up termites. Presently, a 400-pound boar grizzly ambled into view, spotted the sow and cubs, and began moving toward them. The grizzly would probably have succeeded in pouncing on the unsuspecting black bears if the sow had not become aware of my presence and occasionally picked up her head to keep track of my position about 100 yards away. She didn't act overly concerned about me being there, but when she noticed the grizzly 80 yards away she huffed loudly, ran to a tall, limby spruce and followed her cubs up the tree just seconds before the charging grizzly arrived.

The grizzly went right up the tree after the sow and cubs by hooking its paws over the limbs. The grizzly kept pace for the first 30 feet, until the limbs became smaller and thinner, then its progress slowed. Not the black bears. They continued scrambling up to the very top of the tree, putting them about 120 feet above the ground. The big grizzly struggled upwards another 20 feet, but when the limbs began breaking under its weight, it became more concerned with its safety than with the bears above and gingerly climbed down and walked away.

However, it is not always that way when a grizzly chases a black bear up a tree. A ranger in Yellowstone told me that he once watched a grizzly chase a smallish black bear up a fire-killed lodgepole pine. The tree was only 40 feet tall and the black bear could not escape the grizzly, which latched onto the wailing black bear's right rear paw and dragged it out of the tree and killed it.

Black and Grizzly Bears Occasionally Get Along

When trout or salmon congregate in large schools to spawn, black bears descend upon those waters to gorge on the high-protein fish, all the while keeping a keen eye out for any grizzlies, which tend to claim the waters for themselves. At times, a surplus of fish leads to an uneasy peace between black and grizzly, and I've seen both species fishing within 40 yards of each other. But as soon as the grizzly begins to stare at the black bear, it takes the hint and quickly retreats into the brush. A few minutes later, the black bear reappears at the edge of the forest and gauges the grizzly's disposition before venturing into the water.

My friend Bud Cheff lives in the foothills of western Montana's Mission Mountains, which is prime grizzly and black bear country. Bud told me that on his ranch grizzlies are generally intolerant of black bears, and most grizzlies will put the run on any black bear they see. Bud told me, "One time there were four big black bears feeding on the carcass of a steer that had died of natural causes. Suddenly, all four bears scattered. A minute later a big grizzly walked into the pasture and claimed the steer carcass."

At other times, Bud said, grizzlies are surprisingly tolerant of black bears. "We had a dead cow at the edge of a field, and a big grizzly had been feeding on it for two days. The weather was hot, so the grizzly walked about 40 yards away to lie in the shade of a tree. Two black bears showed up and nervously approached the carcass, but the grizzly just laid there and watched them. I guess its belly was too full for it to get up and chase away the black bears."

Being Lower on the Food Chain

The striking contrast in personality between the grizzly and the black bear also serves as an excellent illustration of how each species behaves based on its position in the food chain. For obvious reasons, man is at the top, and even the great grizzly bear's initial reaction is to withdraw from human presence when given a chance. But among the rest of the animal world, the grizzly reigns supreme.

The black bear, on the other hand, is just one notch below the grizzly, but its first reaction is to flee from any unnatural sound, especially in those areas where it is hunted. Many times I've sneaked forward while photographing a black bear that was totally unaware of my presence. But when I stepped on a twig, the bear immediately bolted—without even waiting around to see if the source of the noise presented a danger.

With other animals lower on the food chain, such as deer, beavers, lynx, or coyotes, a black bear will assert its position as a superior predator. When a black bear encounters a lesser predator such as a coyote or deer, it ignores these inferior creatures. In the case of a larger predator, like a lone wolf or mountain lion, a black bear may swagger or walk with stiff-legged-aggressive body posturings that show the lone wolf or lion that the black bear is not intimidated by its presence. Interestingly, the emergence of another wolf instantly puts the black bear on the defensive, and it will retreat to the safety of the forest, where it can climb a tree if the two wolves attack it.

A Black Bear Is Potentially Dangerous

The above analogies should not lead the reader to the false conclusion that the black bear is a wimp. On the contrary the black bear is a powerful animal with the potential to turn from prey to predator in the blink of an eye. Even with a grizzly. A story coming out of Alaska tells of a hiker watching as a 300-pound grizzly chased down and cornered a black bear of equal size. With nowhere to run, the black bear confronted its attacker. During the bloody fight that followed, the black bear was able to get underneath the grizzly and tear at its soft belly, eventually slowing the grizzly and then killing it.

A photographer friend also related a story about a large party of tourists who had stopped at the Headquarters Ranger Station in Yellowstone's Lamar Valley to watch a cow elk nuzzle its newborn calf. In the midst of this idyllic scene, two black bears charged out of the woods and pounced on the calf. They then proceeded to tear apart the calf in front of the horrified tourists. During the calving season, black bears become as predatory as grizzlies and take a fearful toll on newborn elk.

Sows Are Protective of Cubs

Unfortunately, a male black bear, called a boar, considers the cubs of its own kind something to eat. A female, or sow, will immediately huff and send her cubs up a tree and stand guard at its base when a boar appears. Most boars are smart enough to avoid a confrontation, but those foolish enough to move in on the cubs quickly discover that an enraged sow will defend her offspring to the death. If a grizzly comes after her cubs, a sow black bear is protective and will follow her cubs up the tree. And more than one wilderness traveler has recounted a story of a sow black bear fighting to the death against a grizzly in defense of her cubs.

I've encountered many sows with cubs, and most of the time they'll retreat with their young, or send them up a tree while pacing below, huffing and moaning and popping their teeth at me. But at times a sow will abandon her cubs and flee when danger appears. I've twice encountered sows that ran off, leaving their cubs to mill in confusion for a few seconds before scrambling up a tree.

Black Bears and Humans

A sow black bear's instinct to protect her cubs sometimes causes the mother to lose her instinctive fear of humans. Gary Hammond of Helena, Montana, encountered such a sow while working as a wildlife biologist for the U.S. Forest Service in western Montana's Deerlodge National Forest. As Gary moved through a dense stand of alpine fir trees where visibility was only about 15 feet, he heard a muffled woof followed by some whimpering and the sound of claws scraping against bark. Gary guessed it was sow black bear scrambling up a tree with her cubs and started backing away.

Suddenly a 200-pound sow black bear rushed at him, but stopped 10 feet away. Gary yelled and waved his arms and the sow retreated into the dense forest. Gary heard the bear stop about 60 yards away where she began growling and pounding the forest floor with her paws. Gary continued retreating, but then he heard the bear charging through the brush, so he hastily climbed a lodgepole pine. From 20 feet in the air he looked down and saw the sow running in a tight circle around the tree, angrily popping her jaws.

Then the sow started up the tree after him. Gary cocked his right leg and waited until the sow was almost to him, then he kicked her hard in the face. The sow fell out of the tree and landed hard on the ground. Gary breathed a sigh of relief, but it was short-lived. The sow, now angrier than ever, came back up the tree huffing and snapping her teeth. Gary kicked her again, knocking her down, but this time the sow fell only about 6 feet before grabbing onto a limb.

Back up she came, and this time when Gary kicked, his boot hit the bear with only a glancing blow, and she sank her jaws into his right knee. The sow then grabbed his lower leg with her forepaws and leaned out away from the tree, putting her entire weight on his leg. Gary desperately clung to the tree, but the bear's weight was too much and he found himself hurtling downward with the sow's teeth still tightly clamped onto his knee.

Gary remembers landing on the sow's belly with his knees. He blacked out for a few seconds, then jumped up and ran, stopping every 30 yards to listen for the sow. He limped back to his pickup, and a party of land surveyors took him to a hospital, where he was treated for a broken nose and ribs, and multiple cuts and scrapes.

Fortunately, a black bear has an instinctive fear of humans, no doubt the result of thousands of years of hard lessons learned. But the fact remains that, physically speaking, a human is no match for a black bear. Even a smallish 150-pound bear is much more powerful and quicker than the average person. Only our exalted position atop the food chain sends ninety-nine out of one hundred black bears running the other way when they encounter a human.

It is that hundredth bear that demands our attention and respect. Bear attack statistics are sobering. In the five-year period from 1997 to 2002, grizzly bears were responsible for only two human deaths, while black bears killed seven people.

Even more unsettling is the fact that most black-bear attacks are predatory. The majority of grizzly attacks on humans occur when a person surprises a grizzly at close range. Feeling threatened, the grizzly rushes forward to neutralize the threat before retreating. A black bear, on the other hand, may instinctively run away, and then stop to assess the situation. If it decides the human does not pose an immediate physical threat, it may actually advance, though always ready to flee if it feels threatened.

This is exactly how most recorded black bear attacks occur. I recently watched a National Geographic television program of a near-disaster between an amateur cameraman and a black bear. A young man was hiking in a swampy forest when he spotted a black bear and began filming it. The black bear ran away at first, but then came back. When the cameraman yelled, the bear retreated, then returned. Closer and closer the black bear came, and a few times it appeared to me that the only thing that saved the cameraman from attack was that he jumped into a bog while he was retreating from the bear.

Ranger Carlin Kaufman had a terrifying similar experience while on a routine patrol along a popular hiking trail in Alaska's Denali National Park. Carlin began hearing shuffling sounds behind her as she hiked, but each time she looked back she saw nothing. Then she heard another noise and turned to find a large black bear galloping right at her. Carlin yelled and waved her arms, and the bear stopped and began circling her. She started throwing rocks at the bear and several times she saw dust billow from the animal's fur when a rock bounced off its body. Then the bear began stalking her, snarling and showing its teeth.

Now totally spooked, Carlin began swinging her radio at the bear. The bear finally backed off, then came at her again and stopped just a few feet away. "I was absolutely terrified while all this was going on," Carlin recalls. "It seemed like an eternity that I was fending this bear off, but it was actually about thirty minutes. At one point, the bear was so aggressive that I thought I'd be mauled at any moment and when I looked at those huge teeth snarling at me I thought, 'Boy, this is going to hurt really bad.'"

Then Carlin got an idea. She turned her radio to full volume and turned up the squelch. The instant the loud, screaming static ripped through the air, the bear ran off, and Carlin hastily retreated to her pickup a mile away.

Bear Pepper Spray Works on Black Bears

Bear pepper spray works as well on black bears as it does on grizzlies. I've sprayed two aggressive black bears, and each time sent the bruin into a hasty retreat, coughing and pawing at its face as the hot red pepper burned its eyes, mouth and nose, and scorched its lungs. One spring afternoon I was photographing a large boar along a grassy road when the bear suddenly began staring at me. Direct eye contact is considered an act of aggression among predators, so I slowly eased away, but the bear started walking toward me in a stiff-legged gait, another sign of aggression.

Even after I'd reached my pickup, the bear continued forward, so I pulled out my pepper spray and blasted the bear when it approached 30 feet. As the orange ball of airborne pepper engulfed the bear's head, it began gagging and frantically pawing at the air. Instead of running, it stumbled away, no doubt because it could not see well with its eyes burning like fire.

John Fremont, a game warden for the U.S. Air Force in Alaska, has responded to hundreds of black bear complaints from residents at air bases. "Whenever I find a bear rooting around in a garbage can or dumpster," John says. "I just walk right up to it and blast it with the bear pepper spray. A couple times the bears even charged, but every time the bears ran away bawling and coughing and pawing at their faces. And they never came back. That's another good thing about bear pepper spray. It administers adverse conditioning to the bears, and they begin to associate garbage with a painful experience. Which is exactly what I want."

Seasonal Bear Behavior

In spring the black bear is most visible because the weather is still cool (bears are highly intolerant of heat), and it is ravenous from a long winter's sleep. The black bear is a wonderful creature to observe, with its shiny black (or brown or red) coat glistening as it chomps on spring grass and dandelions in early morning and late evening. As the heat of summer increases, a black bear retreats into dense forests or swamps to forage for roots and forbs. At this time of year the black bear is virtually nocturnal and seldom seen, much to the dismay of visitors to our national parks.

One late July afternoon I arrived at the Lower Loop Trailhead in Glacier National Park after a 14-mile hike from its beginning at Logan Pass. I'd started at first light and had seen two black bears and a grizzly the first hour. While I waited for a ride back to my vehicle, I struck up a conversation with a young couple from Kansas. They had driven back and forth in the park for two days and were disappointed they hadn't seen a bear. I sauntered across the road and sat on a stone wall to eat my lunch and enjoy the panorama. I glanced below and was surprised to see a 150-pound brown-colored black bear emerge from the forest. The bear ignored all the traffic above and busied itself turning over rocks and lapping up grubs and termites. I tiptoed back across the road and asked the Kansas couple, "Would you like to see a bear up close?"

They thought I was joking as I led them across the road, but their eyes bugged out when they saw the bear busily turning rocks less than 20 yards below. The young lady, I noticed, was trembling. She later jokingly told me her jitters were partly from excitement and partly from fear. Unfortunately, others came over to see what we were looking at and raised such a ruckus that the bear ran away.

In August when the weather begins to cool and berries ripen, the black bear gorges on the high-sugar fruit to build up an ample supply of fat to take it through five months of hibernation. This is one of the best times to spot black bears, as they wander into openings where chokecherries, blackberries, and huckleberries grow. More than once I've picked huckleberries 100 yards away from a black bear. Each of us was aware of the other, but as long as each stayed a safe distance apart there seemed to be an uneasy truce, allowing bear and man to harvest the sweet berries without incident.

For those hiking along a backcountry trail, it's easy to spot signs of a black bear in the area. Being territorial, a boar will rake its claws down prominent trees, leaving deep gouges in the bark. As a black bear ambles along it is constantly flipping over rocks in search of grubs and termites, so watch for overturned rocks. The biggest termite feasts are found in logs and a bear will literally tear a 2-foot-diameter log to shreds to get at the larvae inside. I so much enjoy reading these signs left behind by a black bear that a day afield is complete for me even if I don't actually see a bear.

View Black Bears at a Distance

The Rocky Mountains are a great observatory for bear lovers. From a prominent point above prime bear habitat in late evening or early morning, your chances of seeing a black bear are excellent, especially in spring, when bears are in the open feeding on grass, or in August, when they invade the huckleberry patches. There's also a chance you'll encounter a bruin traveling along a forest trail. And even if you don't see a bear, it's exciting just seeing bear claw marks on a tree, or overturned rocks and torn-up stumps.

If you should be fortunate enough to see a bear, stay where you are and admire this awesome beast from a distance. Never advance towards a bear. It may be a sow with cubs hidden nearby that you are unknowingly approaching, or it might even be a grizzly. If you want a closer look, bring along binoculars, but don't endanger yourself or the bear by forcing a confrontation.

Hibernation in the Northern and Central Rockies

When the first snows of late fall appear, the black bear actually migrates to a higher elevation where the snow is deeper. There it locates a suitable den under the roots of an overturned tree. Studies have found that some black bears return to the same den year after year. The bear lines its den with grass and leaves and curls up for a long snooze. Snow soon buries the den, and the bear slumbers through the winter months. It is during this period that a pregnant sow gives birth, usually to two cubs. Hairless and not much bigger than a man's fist at birth, the cubs suckle from their sleeping mother and grow quickly.

Not a true hibernator, a black bear will emerge from its den when periodic warm weather sweeps through the high country. By the time a bear finally leaves its den in mid-April, the lower elevations have been without snow for almost a month, and lush green grass is popping up in sunny openings. The bears descend to the lower country and hungrily devour this nutritious early grass.

By now the cubs weigh about five pounds and are fully furred. Cubs are often multicolored. Many times I've seen a brown and black cub, or a brown and blond. I once saw a black, brown and blond cub trailing after a brown sow. A new bear family is a delight to behold: The cubs are constantly at play, stalking and play-fighting as they roll in a furry mass, or biting at each other's tails, and sometimes even jumping on their mother as she grazes on grass or digs roots. The sow takes this abuse for a few minutes before casually swatting the offending cub away.

Hibernation in the Southern Rockies

Only occasional snowstorms that drop a few inches of snow, which melts quickly, occur in the southern Rockies. Other areas receive no snow and temperatures seldom dip below freezing. In spite of these temperate conditions—as compared to 8 feet of snow and twenty below zero temperatures common in the northern Rockies—the black bear of the southern Rockies also hibernates.

With most of their food dried up or exhausted by November, most black bears seek dens under fallen trees or in caves to sleep the winter away. Pregnant females also need a dormant time to nurture their tiny, hairless cubs before they venture out of the den in spring. Boars aren't quite as prone to hibernate through the winter and occasionally leave the den to forage for food during periods of warmer weather. Like their northern cousins, bears in the southwestern Rockies leave their dens for good in early April, when grass and other plants are flourishing.

Species Description

A mature male black bear weighs about 350 pounds in the Rockies, with females rarely weighing more than 250 pounds. Black bears in other areas often weigh much more because of the abundance of food. For instance black bears in Alaska, where berries and salmon are in abundance, often weigh more than 400 pounds, and black bears from Midwestern states have tipped the scales at 500 pounds or more, due to the abundance of high-protein acorns and beech nuts.

Black bears come in a variety of colors, from blond to black. Though black is the predominant color, upwards of 30 percent of black bears in the Rockies are brown in color. A black bear's head is more sloped when seen in profile, its ears are rounded and the eyes are smallish and beady. In addition, a black bear's shoulder line lacks the distinctive hump of the grizzly. Its claws are about 1½ inches long, as compared to 4 inches for a grizzly.

Habitat

Black bears are occasionally found in open areas, especially in spring when the grass first greens up on open side hills. However, black bears prefer the seclusion of dense cover, such as swampy thickets and dark forests, to avoid grizzly bears and man. They also seek this cover to escape the heat. Black bears rarely venture into the open during sunlight hours, possibly because their coats soak up so much warmth.

Black bears also find safety in forested habitat. All black bears, including cubs, are excellent climbers, and at the first hint of danger will scurry up a tree. While it is true that a grizzly can also climb a tree if there are ample limbs to hook its paws on as it pulls itself up, a black bear actually digs its claws into a tree's bark, and I've seen bears scurry effortlessly up 3-foot-diameter trees with no limbs for 50 feet.

Range and Population

Black bears range extensively throughout the Rockies and are present in virtually every type of habitat, from the dense coniferous forests of the northern Rockies to the stunted pinion and cedar forests of the southern Rockies. They are even found in the cactus and desert scrublands of southern Arizona and Mexico.

Black bears are found in great abundance throughout the Rocky Mountain states and Alaska. Arizona has about 3,000 bears, Idaho has 25,000, Colorado has 13,000, Utah harbors 2,000, and Montana has about 20,000 bears. Only Wyoming, which lacks a staple huckleberry crop, has low bear numbers, with only about 800 bears in that state. Alaska, with its abundance of bear food, boasts a whopping 150,000 black bears, and there are about 200,000 in the Canadian Rockies.

Mating

A female black bear goes into heat in mid-June of her third year. At this time, mature males wander long distances seeking a mate. When a receptive female is found, the male woos her with affectionate rubbing and nuzzling. One time I drove around the corner of a forest road in north Idaho and spotted an amorous male and female black bear standing in the middle of the road. The bears stood nose to nose, sometimes nuzzling and at other times playfully biting softly each other's muzzle. So enraptured were the bears they did not notice my pickup easing to a halt just 20 yards away. Then another pickup roared around the corner and chased them off the road. I was disappointed because I had hoped to observe the bears mating.

A female black bear stays in heat for about nine days, and during that period the male will mate with her numerous times, then leave when her estrus cycle ends. After this brief period of togetherness, male and female black bears have nothing to do with each other. When the female emerges from hibernation with her cubs, a male black bear often looks upon them as prey and it is only the fierce protective nature of the sow that discourages a boar from grabbing one.

THE WOLF

From a makeshift blind in a sagebrush thicket 600 yards away, I watched through binoculars as three wolves, one gray and two black, tugged and pawed at the remains of the cow elk they'd killed across the Lamar River in Yellowstone National Park. It had been three days since I'd found the pack feeding on the freshly killed elk, and they'd returned one last time to clean up the carcass, which by now consisted mostly of scraps of meat clinging to the hide and tallowy strips of meat between the ribs.

The leader, called the alpha male, was a pale gray brute noticeably bigger than the others, his supreme standing in the pack recognized at all times. When he walked by the other wolves they crouched submissively or playfully licked his snout.

While the other wolves gnawed at the carcass, the alpha male stood statuelike, staring back across the Lamar River at two cow elk who had brazenly meandered along the opposite river bank 70 yards away and now stared back at him. I guessed the elk's lack of concern grew from the security of being separated from the wolves by the river, which was swollen to near flood stage by snowmelt.

The alpha male left the pack and walked slowly to the water's edge. Logs floated by swiftly in the roiling chocolate-colored waters, but the wolf's concentration on the elk never wavered. He daintily placed a paw in the frigid water, then another. The elk stiffened and began walking away, with an occasional glance back.

The big wolf took another step, and his tail began to float. A second later the strong current swept him downstream. The two elk watched with growing alarm as the wolf, struggling mightily, slowly swam toward them. The animals broke into a trot and were 300 yards ahead of the wolf before he dragged himself from the water and shook a huge plume of water from his shaggy hide.

The wolf loped after them, but the elk, now running, were far ahead. The alpha male sprinted uphill. The elk in the lead ran uphill and out of sight, but the trailing elk swerved downhill toward a low ridge near the river. It was then that I glanced back and noticed the other wolves had disappeared. This lower elk was running along the river when two gray wolves burst over the riverbank, forcing the cow to her left, where she encountered two black wolves sprinting toward her from above.

The elk galloped uphill straight away from the four wolves. The alpha male was waiting, and in an astonishing burst of speed, overtook the cow and leaped onto her neck, sending both wolf and cow cartwheeling. The cow struggled to rise, but the wolf clamped its jaws on the cow's neck and shook its head violently. The cow elk stiffened, then lay still.

The other four wolves sprinted to the alpha male and greeted him with puppy-dog glee. The big wolf stood stoically eyeing a big draw across the river where three other wolves, all females guarding and nurturing the alpha female's newborn pups, were waiting. The alpha male raised his head and emitted a low, mournful howl. Seconds later a faint howl assured him that everything was fine in wolf country.

When the first gray wolves were introduced to Yellowstone in 1995, then to The River of No Return Wilderness in central Idaho the next year, I had my doubts they would survive. Especially in Idaho where the wolves endured a hard release, meaning they were simply released from pens to fare for themselves. The Yellowstone wolves, by contrast, were given a soft release, meaning they were kept in an enclosure and fed native prey for a month before being set free in the park.

I knew that area of Idaho well. It harbored a good elk herd, but its steep, brushy terrain made travel difficult and hazardous, and many a frustrated hunter went home empty-handed when the elk tunneled into the dense brush. What chance, I wondered, would a couple dozen live-trapped wolves from Canada have to survive in such a hostile land? But after watching that Yellowstone wolf pack down the cow elk, I realized that any elk a pack of wolves zeroed in on was a dead animal.

Environmentalists and wolf lovers have hailed the reintroduction of the wolf to the Rockies as one of the great environmental success stories of all time. True, the wolf is back, but such ebullience may be premature, given the proclivity, and the ease, of earlier generations of Americans to eliminate the wolf.

Wolf Genocide

When the Pilgrims landed on Plymouth Rock, the wolf was the most commonly distributed predator in America, efficiently controlling excess populations of deer, elk, and moose. Conflicts arose, and a steady program of genocide extirpated the wolf from all lands east of the Ohio River by 1830. The unsettled prairie country of the Midwest held a healthy wolf population, but the elimination of the buffalo, then the elk, left the land devoid of the wolf's natural prey animals. The wolf began to prey on the livestock of newly arrived settlers and was eliminated from the prairie country.

The remaining wolves retreated to the foothills of the Rocky Mountains, where lush meadows fed by mountain snows provided good feed for herds of elk and deer. The land was also excellent for grazing cattle, and soon big cattle companies moved in, with huge contracts to provide beef to the federal government. For these big companies, even a wolf killing an occasional calf was unacceptable, and what followed became one of the most widespread, and disastrous, environmental calamities in America.

Influenced by the demands of the large cattle companies to rid the land of vermin, western state governments began offering bounties on wolves. Hundreds of thousands of scalps were turned in by wolf hunters, called wolfers. Beginning in 1884, Montana paid bounties on more than 80,000 wolves, while Wyoming tallied 36,000. Fraud among these unscrupulous men was common. Many a wolfer dug pups from their den and kept them in pens, where they bred and furnished a steady supply of wolf scalps.

Not satisfied with these impressive numbers, cattle companies petitioned the federal government to eliminate the wolf because most of the grazing lands were federal. Government officials, their pockets bulging with money from the cattle companies, created the Predator and Rodent Control (PARC) Service.

Poisoning Wolves—and Everything Else

The wolf, being a quick learner, began to shy away from the open areas where it could be shot and also learned to avoid traps. But the wolf still had to eat, so wolfers and PARC employees resorted to poison. With deadly efficiency wolfers and PARC men rode their horses in a gridlike pattern through wolf country, scattering fist-sized chunks of strychnine-laced balls of beef fat. The beauty, excuse the oxymoron, of strychnine is that it has staying power. A teaspoonful of the white powder rolled into a fist-sized chunk of fat quickly kills the first animal that eats it, but this poison is so potent that it also kills the next animal that scavenges the first dead animal, and the next animal that eats the second poisoned animal, and on and on, until the poison is eventually diluted.

A typical poisoning scenario went something like this: A diminutive swift fox comes upon the freshly dropped bait and eats it, stumbles a few steps, writhing in agony, and dies, whereupon crows, magpies, hawks, and eagles descend upon the carcass. Soon all of these creatures are dead. Then a coyote comes along and devours the birds and dies, then maybe a black bear, or a grizzly, or a mountain lion. On and on the deadly chain continues, until a wolf eventually happens by and eats the poisoned carrion, with fatal results.

An astonishing story about the longevity of strychnine that I read in an old history book warrants relating. In 1880 a rancher in southeastern Montana hired an old wolfer to trap and poison coyotes and wolves on his land. The wolfer set up camp in a draw and set out three beaver carcasses laced with strychnine. The poison wiped out the coyotes and wolves—and everything else—in the country. Before the wolfer left, he warned the rancher to keep his dogs away from the area for a couple of years.

The rancher had a very special pet, a greyhound owned by the infamous General George Armstrong Custer that was found wandering among the hundreds of dead at the Little Bighorn battlefield the day Custer was killed. It had been five years since the old wolfer had departed when the rancher rode into the draw to search for a missing cow, with the greyhound tagging along. Near a steep gully, the greyhound walked up to the bleached bones of an ancient beaver carcass left behind by the old wolfer half a decade before. The greyhound licked the skeleton a few times. A few minutes later the dog was writhing on the ground, and ten minutes later it was dead.

The private, state, and government poisoning program was a success. The wolf disappeared from the West, along with every other creature that took so much as a single lick of bait or nibbled on a strychnine-poisoned carcass. Millions of other animals died unintentionally, resulting in an environmental wasteland that makes Rachel Carson's *Silent Spring* seem like a Sunday church picnic.

Through the early 1900s, those few wolves that had miraculously avoided poisoning continued to be picked off by anyone carrying a rifle, and by the midpoint of the twentieth century, the wolf was considered extinct in the West. As each western state upgraded its wildlife agencies to scientifically monitor endangered species ranging from the bald eagle to the grizzly bear, the wolf was left off the list. And why not? The official word was that there were none!

Ghost Wolves

Unsubstantiated wolf sightings continued to trickle in to state wildlife agencies. Bureaucrats jokingly called them ghost wolves and solemnly admonished any caller with the quip, "There are no wolves in the lower states. You probably just saw a big coyote." (A mature coyote weighs about thirty pounds, while a mature male wolf weighs about 125 pounds, and females one hundred pounds.)

But they were wrong. I saw my first "ghost wolf" in the fall of 1974 near the north end of Dworshak Reservoir in North Idaho's Clearwater National Forest. The Floodwood, as it is called, is a vast wilderness consisting of rocky bluffs and unbelievably steep, brush-choked terrain. It's also great elk country. In the murky light of dawn on September 18, I sat on a log and watched two rutting bull elk 300 yards away across a steep ravine lock antlers and battle for the right to claim a harem of eleven cows feeding disinterestedly in a nearby meadow.

The elk suddenly stopped pushing at each other and stood tensely, eyeing the far corner of the meadow, and then bolted. It was then that I heard it, a deep, mournful howl, followed by another. I'd heard hundreds of wilderness sounds, ranging from coyote howls to lion screams, elk bugles to moose grunts. But I'd never heard anything like this. My mind cried, "Wolf!" Still, at that time in my life, I'd never heard a real wolf howl, and this lack of firsthand experience made me doubt my original suspicion. But not for long.

A gray animal trotted into the meadow, and my binoculars focused in on a large canine with pale gray fur, long legs and dished-out face. I'd never seen a coyote like that. Then its mate trotted into the open and any doubt I had evaporated as I studied a magnificent coal-black wolf. The wolves paced back and forth impatiently for a few seconds, then loped after the elk.

I rushed home and phoned the Idaho Fish & Game Department in Coeur d'Alene. I asked to speak to a wildlife biologist, and when the receptionist asked the nature of my call, I blurted, "I just saw two wolves in the Floodwood!"

There was a long pause, followed by the secretary's sarcastic remark, "Were they wearing red hoods?"

Amid the sound of laughter, the wildlife biologist got on the phone and picked up on my Pennsylvania accent. "You're not from around here, are you sir?" he asked.

"Uh, no," I replied, confused by the nature of the question, "but I've lived here four years now and I . . ."

"Well, let me help you out," he interrupted in a condescending tone. "There are no wolves in Idaho. You probably just saw a couple of coyotes."

"Are coyotes black?" I countered before hanging up.

At the time, I was working for the U.S. Forest Service in St. Maries, Idaho. I began asking some of the experienced woodsmen in the area if they'd ever seen wolves and was amazed how many had seen them. Carl Schultz, the crusty old caretaker at Red Ives Ranger Station, an end-of-the-road outpost at the headwaters of the remote St. Joe River country, told me that the previous spring he'd seen two large black wolves trot past the window of his trailer.

John Meshenko, a road locator who spent much of his time in the wild, told me that he'd seen four wolves in the past ten years. He recalled that one day as he was driving along a forest road, a whitetail doe with blood streaming down her flanks bounded across the road in front of his pickup, followed closely by a large gray wolf. The terrified doe scrambled back onto the road and actually sought refuge beside John's pickup while the wolf stood above the road panting. The wolf trotted away, but when the deer bounded off, the wolf again was in hot pursuit.

When I moved to Montana several years later, I continued my amateur sleuthing and soon had a folder full of wolf sightings in Idaho and Montana. In early spring of 1985, Ray Godin, a local logger, called to tell me that he'd found an elk killed by wolves in Gold Creek, a tributary of the St. Joe River. I hurried over there and found the calf elk carcass, ringed by large wolf tracks. I photographed the tracks, using a dollar bill to show their size, before phoning the Forest Service wildlife biologist at the nearby Avery Ranger District, who warily replied that he'd look into it. To my amazement he called two days later and excitedly informed me that they indeed were wolf tracks around the elk carcass. He was the first state or federal official who acknowledged to me the existence of wild wolves in the Rocky Mountains.

Natural Mortality Hurts the Wolf Recovery

Over the next few years, wolf reports increased, but an established natural wolf population never materialized, in part because wolf mortality in the wild is high. The wolf depends on power and speed, and the cunning strategy of pack hunting, to overcome its prey. Take away or inhibit either of these traits, and the wolf's survival becomes tenuous, especially if it does not exist in sufficient numbers to allow the pack to provide for it while it heals. Those individual ghost wolves, in my opinion, all died off when adversity struck.

The hazards of chasing and bringing down large, swift-moving prey animals greatly limit wolf longevity. Wolves in Alaska live barely three and one-half years because of the harsh climate and the danger of attacking the 2,000-pound Alaskan moose. Wolves in the lower states fare somewhat better, living about six years, before an accident (six have been killed by cars and trucks while crossing roads) or a prey animal causes mortality. When officials found a large female gray wolf dead in south central Idaho's Boise National Forest, they initially suspected foul play, but an autopsy revealed the wolf's skull had been crushed, probably from the kick of an elk.

Wolves are even hard on each other. A wolf passing through is often killed by a resident pack, and neighboring packs have been known to fight to the death. Even within the pack an injured wolf is tolerated for only a short time. After a few hunts a lagging wolf begins to lose its status within the hierarchy. The mighty alpha male, returning from a hunt with a limp, will soon be challenged by the beta male and then cast out of the pack. Outcast wolves that continue to follow the pack may be set upon by their siblings and killed.

One of the first female wolves to give birth to pups the first year in Yellowstone was eventually cast out of the pack to roam aimlessly, begging for scraps after the pack had cleaned up a kill. Eventually, even that proximity was unacceptable, and she was killed by other females in the pack.

The Return of the Wolf

A sustained natural wolf reintroduction began in 1986 when a pack of wolves migrated south from Canada and took up residence in Glacier National Park. The next spring this pack produced seven pups, the first documented wolf litter south of the border in more than fifty years. Several lone wolves that had been seen roaming Glacier in previous years joined with dispersed wolves from this original pack to start new packs that ranged beyond park boundaries into areas of northwestern Montana, where wolves were unheard of.

An ebb and flow of fortunes kept the future of this embryonic wolf population in doubt, especially when they ventured into Canada, where wolf hunting is still legal. For instance all members of the Wigwam pack vanished (arbitrarily named to differentiate it from the neighboring Headquarters wolf pack). Shortly after, the Headquarters pack disappeared. Wolf researcher Diane Boyd found five of the bodies and guessed they were probably poisoned.

In the meantime a national survey showed overwhelming support by American citizens for reintroduction of the wolf to our wildlands and parks in the western states, where wolf specialists felt the land could support them. As a result, live-trapped wolves from Canada were released in Yellowstone National Park in 1995, and the next year 30 wolves were introduced into the 27,000-square-mile River of No Return Wilderness Area in central Idaho. Despite early fears and trials, these wolves flourished. A 2004 survey counted 300 wolves in Yellowstone, with another 650 spread throughout Idaho, Wyoming, and Montana. Canada has about 10,000 wolves, with another 7,000 in Alaska.

The Ninemile Wolves

These numbers, however, are deceiving and furnish the potential to lull the public into thinking wolf reintroduction is complete. Nothing could be further from the truth. Enormous problems still plague the reintroduction effort—some of man's making, some the wolf's. Nothing better illustrates this dichotomy as succinctly as Montana's famous, some would say infamous, Ninemile wolf pack.

Ninemile Creek begins as a trickle in western Montana's high country, just south of the Flathead Indian Reservation, and meanders through meadows and heavy forest for 35 miles until it drains into the Clark Fork River 15 miles west of the bustling college town of Missoula. In its upper reaches it's wilderness, but midway down early settlers cleared the forest to provide fields for their livestock. Any wolves back then were quickly eliminated.

When longtime rancher Ralph Thisted went out to mend a fence on a cold January morning in 1990, there hadn't been a wolf in the Ninemile Valley for more than half a century. Ralph spotted a large gray animal standing 60 yards away, watching him. Ralph knew coyotes; this was no coyote. For one thing, it was three times the size, and its legs were way too long, with a muzzle more rounded than a coyote's pointed snout. The animal finally trotted off. When his brother arrived, Ralph announced, "I just saw a wolf."

The wolf, a female dispersed from the Glacier packs, had a history. She'd been trapped and radio-collared south of Glacier National Park, on a ranch where some calves had been killed, though investigators weren't sure if wolves or coyotes had done the killing. The female wolf roamed extensively through the Flathead National Forest, and passed through several settled areas without incident prior to showing up in the Ninemile Valley. The Thisted brothers saw the lone female several times over the next month. Then one day they saw her trot across their lower pasture in the company of a large black male wolf. This wolf had no history and was undoubtedly one of those "ghost wolves" that had been roaming the Rocky Mountains for decades.

Later that spring the pair produced a litter of six pups: three gray and three black. Wolf biologists monitoring wolf reintroduction were excited by this natural reproduction, especially since the adults totally ignored the Thisteds' livestock while rearing their pups. During the summer, the female could be seen teaching her pups how to catch grasshoppers and mice in a nearby meadow, while cattle grazed just 100 yards away.

But in the midst of these encouraging events, tragedy struck. The female's radio collar began emitting a mortality signal. Investigators found her radio collar, cut from her neck by a knife, floating down Ninemile Creek. The female's carcass was never located, and authorities surmised that someone who was against the introduction of wolves shot her.

It's rare for a male wolf to raise pups, but amazingly, the big black male took over the duty of raising the pups, and the crisis seemed resolved, until he was killed on Labor Day in 1990 by a truck while crossing Interstate 90 on his way to a prime deer hunting area at the mouth of nearby Fish Creek. With no adult to protect and feed the pups, they were doomed. Wolf biologists, unwilling to give up on these offspring of two wolves that had integrated themselves well into cattle country, decided to allow the pups to roam the familiar land around the Thisted Ranch and leave deer carcasses for them. Against all odds, the pups survived and grew into handsome subadults by the spring.

Now weighing sixty pounds, the wolves resembled a wolf pack in miniature. In late spring they began to make their first kills, mostly fawn whitetail deer too small and slow to keep up with their fleet-footed mothers. Through the summer Ninemile residents, many whose ancestors had vilified the wolf, were startled to see the young wolves peacefully trotting across their property, oblivious to cows and sheep and horses. This lack of interest in the Ninemile's domestic stock, and the young wolves' very unwolflike tendency to appear in public, quickly won over the majority of folks, with public opinion soaring as high as 90 percent in favor of the wolves. One resident related how he'd watched through his living room window as a wolf caught mice in his pasture barely 100 feet from feeding cows and calves. Another recalled watching the young wolves running helter-skelter through his pasture as they chased down grasshoppers.

A regular procession of wolf biologists and wolf lovers paraded to the Thisted Ranch to observe the pack. Its docile nature and seeming willingness to live among people and livestock prompted one observer to comment, not entirely in jest, that this Ninemile wolf pack might become the seed crop for a hybridized species that refused to identify animals in pastures as prey. In other words, a kinder, gentler wolf.

Unfortunately, that illusion was shattered on a cold morning in March the next spring. The wolves, stirring from slumber under the low hanging boughs of a spruce tree, yawned and stretched and shook a dusting of snow from their coats. Early spring in Montana is a harsh season. The deer and elk young had not yet been born; the weak and old had long ago passed through the wolves' bellies. A hard crust of snow made mousing impossible. Genes long suppressed by an unnatural environment coursed through the wolves' blood, prompting ancient, primal urges for survival. The pack started off at a lope, circled through a thicket in search of a deer or elk, to no avail, and trotted in the direction of a nearby pasture. Later that morning, a rancher found a dead steer in his pasture. A second dead cow was found the next day.

Despite proclamations to the contrary by well-intentioned wolf lovers, the animals in the Ninemile pack were wolves after all. Nature put them on the earth to kill surplus animals and that is exactly what the Ninemile pack did that morning. Anything on four legs is prey for a wolf, and only the intimidating presence of man had kept the young wolves at bay; but with their maturing bodies came maturing instincts, and they did what comes naturally to a wolf. They killed.

Standard repercussions followed. With radio collars attached to their necks, the pack was easy to locate, and the wolves were trapped and shot from a low-flying helicopter, until only a single animal remained. But within a year other wolves moved into the Ninemile Valley when surplus wolves were naturally dispersed from other packs into the region. Eventually, a cow or horse would be killed, resulting in another program of attrition. The early optimism of Ninemile residents, bordering on camaraderie, slowly began to erode as they experienced the inevitable consequences of living among wolves. Resident John Schramm's affable black Labrador retriever, Athea, caught the scent of a female wolf and barked as she chased the coyly retreating animal across their field and into the woods. Lying in wait was the rest of the pack, which quickly surrounded Athea and tore her to pieces.

Another resident just 100 feet from the main Ninemile road watched as his large German shepherd bounded down the driveway to confront a male wolf trotting along the pavement. In a blur the wolf had the dog by the throat and with one vicious shake of the wolf's head, the dog was dead. Even Ralph Thisted's dog was killed by a wolf. House cats disappeared, along with chickens, a pig, a horse, and more cattle.

The only domestic animal that had escaped the wolves' attention was the llama. Word had it that this South American transplant's odd appearance and aggressive, vigilant nature kept wolves away. Misconceptions often die hard, but in wolf country they die quickly. One night the wolves discovered that llama made good eating, so good, in fact, that three more were killed. Planes and helicopters and traps exacted a murderous toll on the offenders.

The llama incidents tipped the scales of public opinion among Ninemile residents firmly against the wolves. The rhetoric was eerily similar to sentiments of the past. Geri Ball, who lost one llama to wolves and had another seriously injured, told a Missoulian newspaper reporter, "I don't feel the government is doing all that they could. They aren't managing them. There were eight calves and a dog killed at one place. Three horses were killed on the Fire Creek Ranch up the road. A farmer lost an 800-pound steer in his corral. Something's got to be done. I'm afraid it will be a child or a jogger next. A moving target is a moving target."

The tragic saga of the Ninemile wolves is sure to continue. A steady parade of city dwellers continues to creep up Ninemile Creek, resulting in less natural prey for wolves and more temptation within fenced pastures and corrals. It's only a matter of time before the helicopters and blazing guns return. Sadly, the above scenario is typical across much of new wolf country. The wolves in the Sawtooth Mountains of central Idaho were drastically reduced from four packs to one after repeated bouts of livestock predation, and several packs in Montana were eliminated after preying on domestic stock. Watching with increasing alarm, officials from neighboring states said, "Thanks, but no thanks," to natural wolf recovery. Recently, three wolves crossed the Snake River into Oregon from Idaho and were trapped and shipped back to where they came from.

When I asked an Oregon wildlife official at a Rocky Mountain Elk Foundation convention if that state had any plans to reintroduce the wolf, his reply was quick and to the point. "Oregon isn't wolf country," he said.

"Where then," I asked, "is wolf country?"

"Anywhere but Oregon," he quipped.

Are Wolves Getting a Bad Rap?

Despite the depredation problems with the Ninemile wolves, statewide tallies kept by the Montana Agricultural Statistics Service show that wolves pose little overall threat to livestock. A severe winter in 1997–1998 reduced deer populations in northwestern Montana, causing wolves and other predators to look to domestic stock more often than in the past. As a result, sixty livestock animals were killed by wolves in one year.

But even those heightened numbers (the previous high was twenty-three) pale in comparison to the depredation of other predators. For instance, domestic dogs killed 1,600 animals in 1995. Mountain lions took another 800. And coyotes killed a whopping 29,000 head of livestock in 1995. That same year, wolves killed only four.

The Future of the Gray Wolf in the Rockies

The U.S. Fish & Wildlife Service currently estimates there are fifty breeding wolf packs in the northern Rockies. Much effort and tens of millions of dollars have been spent to cultivate the wolf's reintroduction as quickly and as widely as possible. Human reaction in many of these areas has followed an unnerving pattern: Initial infatuation with the wolf as its mournful howls echo from the forest, followed by concern when a neighbor's cow is killed, then aversion when a family pet is killed at the back door.

In the meantime, opposing sides are polarized in their rhetoric, with wolf advocates wanting even more wolves and anti-wolf people wanting none. From my experience, the solution lies somewhere in between. The "New West," with its condominiums and ski resorts and gas-guzzling Hummers infringing upon the heart of wilderness, is a far cry from the isolated country where wolves in the past lived in harmony with the land. There simply are not enough backcountry areas where more and more wolf packs can roam and find prey without falling prey themselves to the hazards of civilization. Does that mean that the reintroduction of the wolf is doomed in the Rockies? Not at all, but hard lessons learned in the last few years have shown that the wolf is no respecter of people, or their livestock or family pets.

In many of these fringe areas, where people have infiltrated wilderness, wolf biologists would better serve the overall cause of the wolf by removing any animals that stray into human settlements, thereby avoiding adverse publicity when the inevitable occurs. The Ninemile Valley is a prime example of a place where packs appear and struggle to survive and eventually become desperate to the point of slipping into a corral for, of all things, a llama.

There are still many true wilderness areas in the Rockies, places wild enough to furnish the wolf with prey animals, while insulating it from human encroachment and protecting the wolf from itself. But it can't be in someone's backyard.

Species Description

People sometimes mistake a coyote for a wolf because these two predators are similar in appearance—both species are gray, with a pointed snout and long, bushy tail. However, there is a substantial difference in appearance between the two, beginning with color. Coyotes are always gray, while a wolf's coat may vary greatly, from almost white to black, though the predominant color is gray. This color variation can be seen in a litter of wolf pups and may include every shade between white and black.

The biggest coyote weighs about thirty-five pounds, while a mature male wolf will weigh more than one hundred pounds. A wolf's physique tends to be heavier at the shoulders, which are massive, and the wolf's head is also more rounded and its snout wider. A wolf's paws are very large and allow it to travel over deep snow without floundering. In the spring of 2004, while traveling along the Idaho-Montana border on snowshoes, I came across a very large wolf track. I followed the track for a few hundred yards, and the wolf never did sink into the snow more than a few inches.

Habitat

Wolves prefer isolated habitat where they feel secure, and since man is the only serious threat to their existence, most wolves prefer wilderness habitat far removed from civilization. However, the wolf is not tied to a specific type of forest growth or elevation. Instead it is prey, being primarily large ungulates (deer, elk, moose), that dictate where the wolf will be found. In summer it's usually the subalpine country, where deer and elk congregate to graze on succulent grass and rear their young. In winter they migrate to lower elevations with less snow, and the wolves follow.

Winter is the most dangerous time for the wolf because the pack is often in close proximity to civilization, and it is usually during these winter or early spring months when wolf depredation on livestock occurs. Most of the human animosity towards the wolf is spawned by the instinctive reaction of a wolf when he is hungry and spots a cow, or a horse, or a llama in a pasture and sees it simply as another prey species.

Range and Population

Wolves now inhabit much of the forested regions of western Montana, central and north Idaho, and northwestern Wyoming. A few wolves naturally dispersed from these packs have appeared in Colorado, Utah, Oregon, and Washington, though at this time federal officials have removed these wandering wolves in an attempt to control the burgeoning population.

This is a real problem because wolves are capable of traveling in a stiff-legged trot (which conserves energy) up to 30 miles in a day. Compounding this problem is the fact that most of the areas where these wandering wolves pop up are near civilization, where they often create livestock problems.

The wolf population in the Rockies now stands at about 600—an amazing number considering there was only a trace population a dozen years ago. Montana has about 120 wolves, Idaho harbors about 280, and Yellowstone is home to about 200. Wyoming's wolf population is growing fast and numbers about 50.

The U.S. Fish & Wildlife Service (USFWS), the federal agency responsible for managing the wolf, has begun the process of removing it the wolf from the endangered species list, which means that the wolf in the future will not be fully protected. The USFWS has ordered the states of Idaho, Montana, and Wyoming to draw up management plans for keeping wolf numbers in check, while at the same time protecting livestock and maintaining a stable breeding population of wolves.

Mating

The mating ritual within the wolf pack is unique among predators and highly sophisticated. Within every wolf pack there is a dominant male, called the alpha. All others in the pack are submissive to the alpha male. Among the females there is also a dominant alpha. The hierarchy within the pack then descends to second-in-command and on down to young wolves. Mature wolves keep the younger animals in line with frequent growls and nips to their flanks.

Unlike domestic female dogs, which may come into heat at any time of year multiple times, a female wolf comes into heat in late February. But in wolf country it would be disastrous for every female to come into heat because the pack could not provide for them. Consequently, only the alpha female comes into heat and is mated by the alpha male. The female then digs a den, where sixty days later she produces a litter of four to eight pups. However, there will occasionally be a second female that comes into heat, and she may be mated by other males within the pack. Wolf pups are lovingly attended to by the entire pack, and when the wolves move off to hunt, two or more pack members are left behind to protect the pups until they are old enough to travel with the adults.

THE MOUNTAIN COYOTE

© Brent R. Paull

My entire body trembled as I looked through the eyepiece of the movie camera. Moments before, I'd filmed a large boar grizzly as he ran down and killed a fifty-pound calf elk on the south side of Dunraven Pass in Yellowstone. The frantic mother elk almost became the big bear's next victim when she came to the aid of her baby and narrowly escaped a vicious swipe from the bear's wicked claws.

Now, the bear tore chunks of meat from the carcass. The camera was on a tripod and still recording, so I backed away and luxuriated in the moment. That was when I noticed three coyotes. I threw up my binoculars and immediately noticed that they were excited—turning one way, then another—while they sniffed the air 200 yards down a shallow draw from the grizzly.

They followed the scent trail for 20 yards, then one of them spotted the bear. I expected the coyotes to turn tail and scatter. After all they'd come upon the most powerful beast in the land on a fresh kill.

But these were no ordinary coyotes. These were mountain coyotes.

I hurried to the camera and zoomed in on the trio a second before they streaked toward the grizzly like they were shot out of a cannon. The big bear, now aware of the oncoming coyotes, stepped forward and bounced on stiff forelegs to warn them, but the coyotes didn't slow their charge.

To my amazement the grizzly lost his nerve and galloped for the safety of a dense lodgepole pine forest 50 yards away. The coyotes galloped past the calf carcass and pursued the bear into the timber. A minute later they reappeared and trotted to the carcass. In a half hour they reduced the entire carcass to a pile of bones and hide.

The mountain coyote that inhabits the Rockies is bigger, stronger, and less furtive than its urban cousin. The urban coyote sneaks through hedgerows at night in million-dollar subdivisions on the outskirts of Denver or Phoenix to raid putrid garbage cans or trots along the freeway looking for food thrown from cars.

True, the mountain coyote and the urban coyote are the same species, but in reality the Rocky Mountain coyote looks and acts like its bigger cousin, the wolf. In fact it was just a few generations back that residents in the Rockies often referred to the mountain coyote as a "brush wolf." That's because the mountain coyote often hunts in a pack, is territorial, and looks upon larger game animals as prey.

Mountain Coyotes Prefer Wilderness

A few years back I took an overnight camping trip along the Idaho/Montana border in midwinter to search for wolverine and lynx tracks. Two days before my excursion a storm had dropped almost 2 feet of new snow, bringing the total to almost 6 feet in the high country. The snow was dry and fluffy as powder, and my 48-inch-long trail snowshoes sank more than a foot deep. I entered Trapper Basin, a long, sweeping drainage, heavily timbered at the bottom, but treeless alpine at the top. I shuffled uphill toward a series of subalpine benches where I'd seen both wolverine and lynx sign in past winters.

After a couple hours of hiking and glassing, I spotted two sets of tracks meandering down from the Idaho state line. I guessed the tracks were made by a pair of lynx, because wolverines usually don't associate with each other. I hurried toward the tracks and soon the exertion of trudging uphill in the trail snowshoes had me sweating profusely. With great anticipation I approached the tracks on a bench where spruce and white fir trees provided shelter. I couldn't identify the tracks because they sank into the powdery snow, so I followed them to the base of a large spruce tree, where the snow depth was only a foot. I bent down and voiced my surprise: "Huh, coyotes."

For reasons known only to them that pair of coyotes had picked one of the most inhospitable environments to live. I do have some theories, though, as to why a coyote might choose to eke out a meager existence in the backcountry, rather than tip over garbage cans in people's backyards.

Harkening back to their wolf ancestry, I believe that some coyotes don't like living close to people, where they must eat garbage to survive and be constantly wary, lest someone shoot them for no other reason than for being a coyote. This constant pressure to avoid danger drives certain coyotes to seek relief in the backcountry—even if this harsh environment brings its own form of misery. These wilderness-loving coyotes mate and pass on their preference for wild living to their offspring.

A Mountain Coyote's Diet

A coyote lacks some of the hunting prowess of the bobcat, but makes up for it with a penchant for gobbling down anything edible. Seldom will a bobcat dine on putrid flesh, but a coyote devours it with relish. An old chunk of stiff hide is sniffed by the bobcat and ignored. Not the coyote, which will gnaw on the hide until it becomes pliable enough to swallow.

During hunting season coyotes roam extensively through the backcountry seeking gut piles left by big game hunters, and they regularly patrol remote campgrounds and specific sites where hunters have discarded animal hides in the past. And like the wolverine, mountain coyotes often roam the remote avalanche areas where they search for winter-killed sheep and goats.

That's not to say that mountain coyotes are not good hunters. On the contrary, they are excellent mousers, even in deep snow, where they hunt mice and pack rats that dig their way up to daylight when the snow gets too heavy. They'll sit patiently for hours in the shadow of a tree and wait for a mouse or squirrel or pack rat to scurry across the expanse of white.

The coyote bounds after its prey, but a mouse often disappears under the snow before the coyote gets there. The coyote leaps into the air and dives into the snow where the mouse disappeared, digging furiously to uncover the rodent before it escapes. More often than not, the mouse flies though the air in the plume of discarded snow and scurries away without the coyote seeing it.

A coyote's paws are narrow and sink into the snow, but it still finds success even hunting the speedy snowshoe hare by using a very wolflike hunting tactic: pack hunting. Many times I've studied tracks in the snow that revealed where a coyote had entered a snowshoe-hare thicket and chased up a hare, which easily outdistanced its pursuer. But in so doing the snowshoe hare ran right into another coyote lying in wait at a strategic spot.

Coyote Pack Hunting

The aggressive nature of the mountain coyote may be the result of its close association with the gray wolf, which usually doesn't tolerate coyotes living near a den where pups are being reared. Wolves either chase the coyotes out of their territory or kill them outright. Only the most aggressive coyotes can withstand a hostile wolf. Having experienced firsthand the effectiveness of a wolf pack's swarming assault, mountain coyotes often employ this wolfish tactic to hunt larger prey animals such as deer, small elk, caribou, bighorn sheep, and mountain goats. A lone coyote may not be able to take down a mature deer, but a pack of coyotes can, and will, regularly kill mule and whitetail deer.

I once watched a single coyote chase a whitetail doe upstream along the East Fork Bitterroot River in the Anaconda-Pintlar Wilderness. Five minutes later the doe bounded back downstream, with the coyote still far in the rear. Fifteen minutes later the doe ran upstream again, though I didn't see the coyote. The last time I saw the doe, she was running back down the river as fast as she could, but her mouth was agape and her tongue hung down, and two large coyotes were gaining on her.

Coyote packs also take a substantial number of deer fawns and elk calves. In Yellowstone in the spring, I've seen coyotes in groups of two or three slipping through sagebrush flats, where cow elk conceal their calves before they wander off for feed and water. By the way the commonly held belief that newborn fawns and calves are odorless is not true, and coyotes and other predators can detect the scent of nearby newborns.

One spring I was asked to film a few sequences of newborn white-tail deer fawns in a wilderness setting. I traveled to the foothills of the Swan Mountains south of Glacier National Park, to a creek bottom where I'd seen several newborn fawns in the past. Two hours after I began searching, I discovered a single tiny hoof and small patch of spotted hide, and coyote droppings with hair in them. Then I found where another fawn had been killed by coyotes, and another, and another. I found six fawn kills before I finally spotted a healthy fawn hidden behind a log by its mother.

A coyote pack can be a force to be reckoned with, as I discovered watching those three coyotes as they drove the grizzly away from its kill. A single coyote may not be much of a threat to a large predator such as a bear or lion, but two or three coyotes have the potential to intimidate these animals. That's because a coyote is extremely quick, and a larger predator usually lacks the speed and quickness to pounce on a coyote.

Three coyotes, intermittently circling and nipping at a bear or a mountain lion, will quickly unnerve it and force it to flee.

The exception is the wolf. Coyotes in wolf country have surely been bullied by the resident wolf pack, and even a single wolf on a kill intimidates a pack of coyotes. And since wolves usually hunt in packs, the coyotes know that the rest of the wolves cannot be far away.

Mountain Coyote Range

Coyote range in the Canadian Rockies extends to the very northern edge, where mountains and forest give way to tundra. Undoubtedly, coyotes would also fare well in this habitat, but the lack of cover for hiding and escaping from the wolf makes life impossible in this treeless land. Coyotes in the northern Rockies exist under brutal winter conditions, where the temperature commonly dips to twenty degrees below zero and snow builds to several feet each winter. At night, when the temperature drops well below zero, a mountain coyote digs a quick burrow in the snow and then curls up for a comfortable night's sleep. Otherwise, a coyote simply curls up under a tree and covers its face with its thick tail.

Mountain coyotes roam through all the Rocky Mountain backcountry below the Canadian border, from Idaho and Montana south through Colorado, Wyoming, and Utah, and into northern New Mexico and Arizona. These states also experience harsh winter conditions at higher elevations, and the mountain coyote exists much like its northern cousin.

South of the Mogollan Rim in northern Arizona and Santa Fe in New Mexico, winter snow levels drop due to more temperate weather. Mountain coyotes fare better than their northern kin and must endure only a few inches of snow, with bare ground often showing between storms.

Predation on Coyotes

The reintroduction of wolves into Yellowstone National Park drew national attention, and eager journalists sought any wolf-related story that sounded intriguing. Someone started a rumor that these early wolves were pitted in a life-or-death struggle with resident coyotes for control of the park's prime hunting grounds. The story was half correct. Indeed, there was a struggle, but it was very one-sided.

The gray wolf, at one hundred pounds or more, outweighs the coyote three times over. True, coyotes are quicker and more elusive—but not by much, especially when the wolf employs its cunning.

A typical coyote/wolf turf war goes something like this: A wolf pack migrates into a valley and takes up residence. An uneasy truce ensues between coyote and wolf until the first wolf litter is born. The urge to protect and provide for their young drives the wolf pack to declare all-out war against every coyote in their territory. When not hunting prey, the best wolf hunters roam areas where coyotes lurk, and employ pack hunting methods to surround and kill any coyote they encounter.

Wolf packs also zero in on coyote dens. When a den is located, the wolves descend upon it and dig furiously until they reach the pups, which are immediately torn apart. Some wildlife biologists initially feared the coyote would disappear from Yellowstone, but wolf country is remote and vast. There's plenty of room for both coyotes and wolves, but the wolf will not tolerate competition close to its den or favorite hunting areas.

It is within this tenuous social structure that mountain coyotes exist. They may not have to fear man's bullets like their urban counterparts, but they must be ever-vigilant to avoid the wolf pack. Where wolves are plentiful, coyotes take great care to locate their dens in dense cover, which is generally avoided by the wolves. In Yellowstone's Lamar Valley, where two wolf packs exist, coyotes often den near human settlements or well-traveled roads.

The Howl of the Mountain Coyote

At any time during the night, a pack of coyotes may erupt with a cacophony of strangled, musical calls. These howls may signify the culmination of a successful hunt or may be the coyotes' way of saying, "Here am I;

where are you?" But as I lie in my sleeping bag, staring at the stars and listening to the coyotes howling all around me, I like to think that they're simply saying, "We're still here."

Species Description

Coyotes and wolves are similar in that both are wild members of the dog family. But for an experienced observer, the difference in appearance between a coyote and a wolf is pronounced. A wolf is at least three times the size of a coyote, and comes in colors ranging from white to gray to black. Coyotes, on the other hand, are varying shades of gray. And unlike the wolf, with its more rounded muzzle and face and smallish, round ears, a coyote's face is narrow, with a pointed snout and tall, pointed ears. Another easy way to tell a coyote from a wolf is to watch their tails when they trot. A wolf carries its tail straight out, while a coyote's tail is held low, or tucked between its hind legs.

In the northern Rockies most mountain coyotes tend to be more light gray, or silver gray in color than farther south, with an almost white belly. This is somewhat of a curse because white-bellied coyotes are always in demand in the fur industry, and hunters and trappers often probe the edges of the wilderness to claim these prized pelts. The good news is that the coyote is an extremely wary and cunning animal, and very few hunters or trappers experience success with any regularity.

In the central Rockies, a coyote tends to be dark gray in the back and shoulders, with more red and brown on the legs and belly. In the southern Rockies, a coyote's fur thins out because the weather is not as cold, and its legs and belly have more red to blend in better with its environment.

A mature male mountain coyote weighs about thirty-five to forty pounds, though a few specimens have weighed upwards of fifty pounds, and one giant coyote tipped the scales at seventy-four pounds. Females weigh about thirty pounds or less.

Habitat

Mountain coyotes prefer dense forest or heavy brush to conceal their movements and avoid predators, but they also like to seek out open vistas where they have a good view of the country below—for prey or predators, such as the wolf. Unfortunately, the wolf often dictates where the coyote will live, banishing its smaller relative to the more remote corners of the wolf pack's home range.

Range and Population

A coyote's home range is usually about 3 miles, but can be much smaller if there is an abundance of food. Within this range the coyote moves between favorite hunting areas, such as isolated meadows teeming with mice, or brushy areas where hares or pack rats make their homes. All the while, the opportunistic coyote keeps watch for larger prey animals such as deer, young elk, or bighorn sheep. The coyote also relishes carrion, so its nose is always in the air, hoping to catch the odor of something dead.

Trying to tally the coyote is like trying to count the stars. They are too many! Biologists guess there may be as many as one million coyotes roaming the Canadian Rockies, with another two million living in the Rocky Mountains south of the Canadian border and into Mexico. This is a staggering number, considering the many millions of dollars spent annually by state and federal hunters and trappers to control the coyote.

Mating

Coyotes have endured centuries of human genocide, having been shot, trapped, and poisoned at a cost of many millions of dollars. The result? There are more coyotes today than ever before. That's because the coyote is a survivor, and its breeding habits reflect this. When coyotes are killed off in large numbers—during government hunting, trapping, and poisoning programs—females produce litters of a dozen or more pups. As a result, coyote control programs that claimed great success in the form of coyote scalps instead prompted an explosion in coyote numbers.

When times are good and coyote numbers threaten to overpopulate their range, coyote litters drop to two or three pups. In times of famine, females often don't drop litters at all, and sometimes a malnourished female will kill her newborn pups.

Breeding season begins in late winter, usually March, when the female coyotes come into heat. One-year-old females are capable of bearing pups, though yearling males normally don't mate. Unlike the strict social structure of the wolf pack, where only the alpha male and female couple, coyote mating season is a free-for-all. Any mature male coyote can, and will, mate a female when she comes into heat. At this time coyotes often congregate in packs of a dozen or more. One or two dominant males chase away lesser males and mate any females. But when they are distracted, lesser males slip in and mate lesser females.

The gestation period is about sixty-three days. During this time, the female digs a den and in late April gives birth to sightless, hairless pups. After ten days the pups' eyes open, and within weeks they are playing outside the den. In two months the pups are weaned and strong enough to follow the pack on hunting forays.

Life for a coyote pup is hazardous, and only about one in four survives its first year. Other predators such as wolves and wolverines kill them, as do mountain lions, bobcats, and lynx. Eagles also take a heavy toll on pups. In retrospect it's understandable why nature allows unregulated reproduction between coyotes.

THE MOUNTAIN LION

W ith less than a minute to live, the big mule deer buck threw up his head. A snapped branch had alerted him, and he tensely surveyed the forest ahead for danger. The ground was free of brush, with nothing but a small dead tree 30 yards away to his right. The buck sniffed the air; the scent of pine needles and decaying wood registered in his olfactory nerves. Nothing that he could see or smell was amiss.

With only a half minute left in his life, the buck started forward, then paused. A sixth sense held him back, urging him to flee, but he was tired and hungry. Up in the alpine country above tree line, where the mule deer spends summer and fall grazing on fresh grass, he'd been the dominant buck. During the rut he'd eaten little and burned up precious fat reserves battling other bucks for the right to mate the does.

When heavy snow began to fall in the high country, the mule deer herd had moved down to the heavy forest below, where there was less snow and more feed. But the strange land made the big buck nervous because he was accustomed to the security of the alpine country, where the cover was scant, and he could easily spot a predator and escape in leaping bounds.

With mere seconds to live, the buck took one furtive step forward, then another. A red squirrel barked to his left, and he snapped his head in that direction. Out of the corner of his eye, he caught a tawny blur coming at him and instinctively leaped back and bounded for the safety of the creek. The water was in front of him, and he was gathering his feet for one mighty leap when a powerful impact sent him flying through the air. The instant he hit the ground, daggerlike claws sunk deep into his neck and powerful jaws clamped onto his throat. The buck struggled to rise, but the suffocating hold quickly paralyzed him, and within seconds he slipped into oblivion.

The above drama was pieced together from mountain lion and deer tracks I found in a snowy creek bottom near the Great Burn Wilderness along the Idaho/Montana border. A deer leg and antlers sticking out of the mound of scraped-up twigs and pine needles told the rest of the story.

The Unseen Deadly Predator

The mountain lion is the silent hunter who lurks through the Rocky Mountains, seldom seen by man and seen usually too late by its prey. Unlike the grizzly bear, with a diet ranging from grass to carrion, the mountain lion snorts from its nostrils the odor of putrid flesh. And while the wolf needs help from its own kind during the hunt, the lion is a solitary hunter that survives by catching and killing some of the most wary and elusive animals in the world.

The efficiency of the mountain lion is astounding. Studies have found that eight out of ten lion hunts are successful. The African lion, by comparison, finds success only once in every ten hunts. No doubt the mountain lion's penchant for hunting alone helps its efficiency because a single animal is far less likely to be detected than three or four.

The mountain lion's success as a hunter can be attributed not only to its stealth, but also to its physical attributes. Its body is long and lean and built for speed, but its legs are disproportionately short, which keeps its profile close to the ground and less likely to be spotted by a sharp-eyed deer. Short legs also provide a remarkable initial burst of speed that can be best described as a blur. A mountain lion's head is small, and its ears stubbed, which allows it to peek above a rock or log without being seen.

But make no mistake, a mature mountain lion is a powerful beast capable of killing prey several times larger. Mountain lions routinely kill full-grown elk, even bulls that weigh upwards of 800 pounds. My friend, Larry Bennet, told me that he was hiking along a snow-covered ridge in western Montana's Bitterroot Mountains on a cold December morning when he noticed a disturbance in the snow a short distance below. Larry skidded down the steep slope and found tracks where it appeared that a mountain lion had bounded down the slope and attacked a large elk. The lion and elk had skidded 100 feet down the side hill, before the elk got to its feet and ran for about 40 yards before being caught. The desperate struggle continued as cat and elk skidded down toward a creek bottom, but now splashes of blood dotted the snow. Larry followed the skid marks to a dense thicket of spruce trees where the ground flattened out.

He peeked into the thicket and spotted the carcass of a mature five-point bull elk. Larry eased forward and laid a bare hand on the elk's shoulder. It was still warm, and only a small portion of the inside of one ham had been eaten. The cat was probably watching him from the depths of the thicket—nervous, but impatient to reclaim its hard-earned kill. Larry backed out of the thicket and hurried away, feeling fortunate to have witnessed the aftermath of such a titanic battle between predator and prey.

How could a mountain lion, probably weighing no more than 150 pounds, kill a mature bull elk that outweighed it by hundreds of pounds? The answer is strength. A mountain lion's jaws possess tremendous biting power, evidenced by the fist-sized muscles at the end of each jaw. A set of forepaws, with formidable 1½-inch-long claws that can rip through thick hide and rake flesh to the bone, complete the lion's weaponry. They're needle sharp and easily sink deep into the prey's hide to furnish a death grip while the lion finishes off its prey with its powerful jaws.

How a Lion Hunts

A mountain lion's hunting territory may be as small as 20 square miles in forested areas where prey animals are plentiful, or as large as 500 square miles in desert habitat were game is scattered. It's been my experience that lions roam extensively, no doubt because prey animals quickly leave an area when they become aware of a lion in the vicinity. Several times I've discovered game-rich pockets where deer were numerous, but within a few days they became devoid of animals after a lion made a kill.

The mountain lion hunts solely by sight, often traveling along ridges or seeking prominent high points to survey the area for prey. When a lion spots a deer, it quickly assesses the terrain ahead and checks the wind direction before slipping forward on the downwind side. Using its low profile to great advantage, the lion uses bushes, logs, even a shallow depression in the ground to quickly move within 100 yards of the deer.

The lion then begins stalking forward, flitting between patches of cover whenever the prey animal lowers it head to feed, and freezing in midstride when the deer raises its head. At 50 yards the lion creeps forward with its belly scraping the ground. At 30 yards the lion is within striking distance but waits for the deer to lower its head or look away before it charges. By the time the deer is alerted, the lion is usually halfway to it and moving at high speed. Most chases end quickly, with the lion swatting at the deer's flanks to knock it off stride, then leaping upon its neck and biting down on the throat, paralyzing the deer and killing it within seconds. If the deer escapes the lion's initial charge, this fleet-footed prey stands an excellent chance of escaping—as evidenced by several whitetail and mule deer I've observed with scars on their flanks.

A lion can easily bring down prey the size of a deer with a single bite or swat, but an elk is too big for even a large lion to simply smack on the flanks and knock down. Instead, a lion attempts to pounce on an elk's neck and use its weight to force the struggling animal into a nosedive. While the elk is down and struggling to rise, the lion kills it quickly by crushing its windpipe with it powerful jaws. One big advantage for the lion is that elk are much less wary than the furtive deer because they have fewer predators to fear.

However, an elk hunt may evolve into a drawn-out, hazardous ordeal. Larry Bennet related to me that he once tracked an elk that was being followed by a lion through a snowy forest. Larry was dumbfounded when the lion's tracks suddenly disappeared, and began to wonder if the lion had climbed a tree. Then he noticed that the elk had begun to run. After he had followed the elk's tracks for 30 yards, the lion tracks reappeared in the snow. The lion had been riding on the elk's back! The elk had somehow dislodged the big cat and escaped.

A Desperate Fight to Save a Lion

I learned firsthand the strength of this great cat a few years ago, when a local rancher who was snaring coyotes that were killing his calves called one afternoon. He blurted out that he had a large male lion in a snare and asked if I could somehow release it unharmed. My son, Tony, and I drove up a snow-covered forest road and parked at a wide spot where the road's cut bank was about 6 feet high. Above the bank was a dense growth of pine saplings, and sitting in that thicket was a large male lion, a twisted steel cable cinched tight around his neck. Tony pulled out a pair of wire cutters while I hastily fashioned a forked stick from an alder bush. The forks of this stick were stout—about an inch in diameter—because I wanted something hefty enough to hold the lion down once I pinned it to the ground.

The lion rose slowly as we cautiously approached him. A rumbling growl came from deep in his throat. In the blink of an eye the animal leaped at me, and I felt the unsettling rush of wind as his daggerlike claws ripped through the air close to my face. Only the steel cable stopped the lion from getting at me.

I jammed the forked stick against the lion's neck and pushed hard, but couldn't budge him. In a blur the lion reached down and bit the stick in half! We retreated and I fashioned another forked stick, but the lion bit that one in half also. Then he bit down on the stick, and I pulled with all my strength, but could not yank that stick out of the cat's mouth.

Round and round we went: the lion spitting and snarling and trying mightily to get at us, held back by nothing but a few thin strands of wire. Tony circled behind the cat and grabbed it by the tail while I occupied it with yet another forked stick. Several times the lion narrowly missed clawing us, but after an hour of nonstop mayhem he began to tire, and we were soaked in sweat. I finally succeeded in pinning the lion's neck to the ground with the forked stick. While the lion was preoccupied chewing the stick and swatting at me, Tony bravely slipped behind the cat and cut through the cable.

Tony and I backed toward the pickup, certain that the cat, once he realized he was free, would bound into the forest. Instead the lion crouched and glowered. Then it came for us, slow at first, but its pace increased at we scrambled down the road's cut bank. In the safety of the pickup, we turned back to see the lion at the edge of the cut bank, tail twitching, yellow eyes boring into us. It finally turned and slowly stalked off.

Lion Prey Varies

Lion prey varies with each region. In the southern Rocky Mountains, which takes in Mexico and the southern half of Arizona, New Mexico, and Nevada, desert-dwelling mule deer and javelina are plentiful in the rocky arroyos and box canyons, and the lion preys heavily upon these thirty-pound pigs and smallish deer. But the lion is also a good climber and takes a heavy toll on desert bighorn sheep. In fact the desert bighorn is in danger of disappearing from some of its haunts because of heavy predation by lions.

In the central Rockies, which includes the northern portions of Arizona, Nevada, New Mexico, and Utah, whitetail deer, the desert Coues deer, the larger Rocky Mountain mule deer, and bighorn sheep comprise a large portion of a lion's diet. But now larger ungulates, such as elk and moose, are also available.

In the northern Rocky Mountain states of Wyoming, Idaho, and Montana, both whitetail and mule deer are important prey animals, but it also preys upon bighorn sheep, elk, and moose when the opportunity arises. Further north into Canada, mountain lions also hunt stone sheep, Dall sheep, and caribou.

The risk of injury to a mountain lion increases in relation to the size of the prey; and given the choice, the lion avoids larger animals. In a study of mountain lions in western Montana, researchers discovered that upwards of 90 percent of the lion's diet was the whitetail deer, even though both deer and elk were plentiful.

That's not to say that an elk is too much for the average lion to tackle. Lions are efficient killers and readily prey upon elk, but these 600- to 800-pound animals also have the potential to seriously harm an attacking cat. If the elk bolts before the cat can sink its claws into its neck and wrestle it to the ground, the lion may be kicked, stepped on, or rolled over. Such an injury may not be serious, but could eventually cause the demise of the cat. A lion with an injured paw or bruised ribs will surely be affected on its next hunt, and when pursuing the whitetail deer, a lion that is slowed down even slightly will surely fail in the hunt for this fleet-footed animal.

There is even some evidence that certain lions become adept at hunting elk and actually prefer these larger prey animals. A lion research team tracking a 120-pound radio-collared female with two yearlings in

Montana noted that half the lion's kills were elk. One day in late March, the team tracked the lion into some bottom land along the foothills of the Rockies, where elk were concentrated while waiting for the snow to melt in the high country. The researchers discovered six dead cow elk killed by the female lion over a span of two days. Very little was eaten from each elk, and the researchers guessed that the female was probably teaching her cubs to hunt elk. It would be their last hunting lesson because the mating season was about to begin, and the female would soon be in the company of a mature male who would chase away the yearlings, forcing them to fend for themselves.

A mature bull or cow moose is a daunting task for any lion, though a calf or yearling, at about 400 pounds, is fair game. However, I was recently shown a friend's home video clip of a female lion with cubs feeding on a full-grown cow moose. The carcass was huge and dwarfed the female.

Normally, a lion kills only what it eats. Prey the size of a deer or bighorn sheep will sustain a mountain lion for about seven to ten days. A larger elk may last two weeks or more. The condition of the carcass has a lot to do with how long the lion feeds on it. In summer, when meat spoils and becomes rancid after about five days, a lion will abandon a kill, even though a large portion remains uneaten. Lions simply will not eat rancid meat unless they are starving. When the weather cools and the meat remains fresh longer, a lion stays close by and feeds repeatedly on its kill, sometimes until nothing remains but bones and hide. One radio-collared female lion killed a cow elk in winter and fed on the carcass for three weeks.

The lion is an opportunistic hunter, and when the chance arises for an easy kill, it can't resist the temptation. I once slipped into a creek bottom in northern Idaho where whitetail deer were concentrated due to deep snow in the high country. I soon found a lion kill that had been abandoned. When I scraped away the twigs and spruce needles, I found that a whole rear ham and both shoulders of the whitetail doe were uneaten. I continued less than 50 yards before I found another kill, this time with half the carcass eaten. In all I found three more lion kills in that creek bottom; I guessed that the female, while lazing in a thicket near a deer trail after feeding on her first kill, took advantage of an easy opportunity when another whitetail ambled along.

One of the most amazing lion incidents I've ever heard of concerning an opportunistic lion occurred at Northwest Trek, a well-known wildlife park nestled in the dense forest 30 miles south of Seattle. The park features many wild animals, including an excellent mountain lion exhibit with three lions. Nearby is a petting zoo for children. One morning, a caretaker noticed a goat missing from the petting zoo. Searchers found the partially eaten carcass tucked under a log. Officials wondered how one of their lions could have escaped its enclosure, killed the goat, then returned to the enclosure. In truth, a passing wild mountain lion had spied the domestic animals behind the 8-foot-tall chain-link park fence and couldn't resist the temptation for an easy meal. The lion had scaled the fence in the night, killed the goat, and returned to the wild. Fearful of the danger to the public, officials brought in a hound hunter who treed and killed the lion.

A Starving Lion Is Dangerous

When prey animals are in ample supply, the lion is truly a wilderness ghost, rarely seen or even thought of, but when deer and elk become scarce, a lion may leave the security of its wilderness home and venture down to the foothills in search of alternative food sources, such as livestock or even family pets. Every year stockmen throughout the Rocky Mountain states lose scores of yearling cows and calves to lions. Of course the offending lion usually pays the price for leaving its backcountry lair when the rancher sends lion hunters with hounds to tree and kill the cat.

Sheep ranchers hate the lion because it occasionally preys on sheep. But in defense of the lion, most sheep predation occurs when large flocks of sheep are herded onto federal grazing allotments in the high country.

To a lion, a sheep resembles a stupid deer and becomes easy prey. One terrified, milling flock in Nevada lost fifty-nine sheep in one night to a single lion.

Starvation will occasionally drive the mountain lion to extraordinary pursuits. Emaciated lions have been known to slip into backcountry settlements and take up residence under an abandoned house. It's not long before the local dogs begin to disappear, then the house cats. Seldom will a mature male lion fall into such a desperate condition, but occasionally a female with kittens will fail in her hunts and sneak near a rural home and kill the family dog.

My friend Steve Crabb lives in the country in the foothills of the Bitterroot Mountains of western Montana. One morning his wife, Cheryl, came running into the house and yelled, "Steve, get your gun! There are two lions out front after the dog!"

Steve, thinking his wife was joking, sauntered to the front door, where he found two smallish lions closing in on his dog, which sat whining and cowering on the front porch. Steve yelled and threw a shoe at the cats, who eyed him sullenly for several seconds before sulking back into the forest.

When Steve called the local game warden, his request to have the cats eliminated was dismissed with the quip, "That's the kind of thing you're going to have to put up with if you choose to live in the woods in lion country."

The main culprit in these dangerous forays is the young lion, usually a yearling chased away by the female before she has her next litter. A sixty-pound yearling may not be big enough or a good enough hunter to catch a deer or elk. These young cats are also harassed by the bigger males and chased out of their home territories to roam strange new country that may not have much of a prey base. At this point a starving young cat will resort to feeding on carrion, and in its desperate search to find anything to fill its grumbling belly, may turn to extraordinary actions such as stalking a family pet.

Mountain lion

Ermine with rabbit

Lynx with snowshoe hare

Bobcat with rabbit

Grizzly bear

Black bear with kill

Ed Wolff

Bobcat stalking beaver

Gary Holmes

Gary Holmes

Predator-chewed elk bones

Mountain Lion Versus Man

For the desperate lion that ventures close to civilization, there is only one other animal easier to prey upon than the domestic dog or cat: humans. In the past one hundred years, ninety-five lion attacks on people have been recorded. Most disturbing is the statistic that most have occurred in the last twenty-five years.

Wildlife biologists believe that three factors have contributed to this sudden surge in lion attacks on humans. Lion populations throughout the Rocky Mountain states have risen steadily as deer and elk herds have increased. Today, lions are in abundance from Chile in South America to the Yukon in Canada. It's difficult for biologists to count these secretive animals, but a conservative estimate puts their numbers at about 50,000.

Some states keep their lion populations in check through limited hunting with hounds, while others, such as Washington, have banned the practice, which essentially eliminates hunting for this secretive predator. California has banned mountain-lion hunting outright. The unfortunate result in these two states has been a startling rise in complaints from folks losing pets to lions, and from terrified homeowners who look out the kitchen window and spot a lion under their carport. In California mountain lions have attacked and killed several women and children since the hunting season was eliminated.

Another major factor in lion/human conflicts is the encroachment of civilization. Folks fed up with the rat race of the city have moved to western states en masse to carve out a secluded homestead (complete with a $500,000 log house) in the woods. In other areas ski resorts have been built right in the heart of the backcountry. Recently one of these ski resorts in Montana offered summer nature outings. A group of six-year-old boys, led by a teenage chaperone, were hiking single file just beyond the ski lodge when a young lion sneaked up behind the group and grabbed the last child by the neck. The cat was pulling the youngster into the brush when the teen leader beat it off the child.

Most of these newcomers to lion country are woefully unaware of the rules of proper behavior. The first thing they do is put out feeders to bring deer to the woods behind the house. Soon a small herd of whitetail or mule deer appear each evening for handouts, much to the glee of the wildlife lovers—and the neighborhood mountain lions. A simple rule of thumb in lion country is this: Where there are deer, there are lions.

When you have deer feeding in the backyard, and lions hunting those deer literally in the same place where kids scamper in play, trouble follows. Western newspapers every year print disturbing stories of lion attacks on youngsters. A few years ago a young lion sprang from a thicket near a rural home in western Montana and attacked a five-year-old boy in his backyard. The lion dragged the body into the brush, where it was partially consumed. Authorities brought in a hunter with hounds. The lion, a yearling, was quickly treed and killed.

How to Avoid a Lion Attack

Unfortunately, not all aggressive lions are found in areas of human encroachment. Though normally fearful of humans, the mountain lion remains a lethal predator; its' primary instinct, like all the big wild cats, is to stalk and attack. Several years ago I had an unsettling encounter. I was pushing through knee-deep snow along a Forest Service trail deep in the wilderness of northwestern Montana the last week in November when I spotted a large mountain lion walking parallel to me through the forest about 60 yards away. At first I was excited to see the animal. I've had the privilege of seeing ten other lions in the wild, but a sixth sense told me this one was different. I hoped the lion was just passing in the same direction, but when I slowed, the lion slowed. When I hurried, the lion hurried, though it acted unaware of my presence.

I lost sight of the big cat in the dense forest and a wave of relief swept over me. Maybe it had moved off. I was startled to see it lope across the trail 40 yards ahead.

I tentatively approached a bend in the trail, hoping for the best, but expecting the worst. I got the worst. The cat was crouched beside a log about 30 feet from the trail. His ears were laid back, yellow eyes balefully glaring at me. I knew that if I traveled the backcountry long enough, something like this might happen. I had long ago prepared for such an encounter. Though I carried no gun, I was not defenseless.

I slowly slid a fifteen-ounce can of bear pepper spray from its holster. The cat's body tensed, and he bunched his feet. That was enough for me. A loud blast of pepper spray shot forward in a huge orange ball and engulfed the cat. It leaped 6 feet into the air, snarling and pawing at its face. The lion hit the ground running and disappeared in a blur.

I recently read a chilling newspaper story about a hundred-pound mountain lion that killed and ate 35-year-old Mark Jeffrey Reynolds while he was riding on a southern California wilderness bike trail. The next day the lion attacked and very nearly killed Anne Hjelle before other cyclists drove the cat off her. I have to wonder how differently these stories might have ended if the victims had been carrying pepper spray, because lions are especially sensitive to its instant burning effects.

Your chances of ever experiencing such an unnerving encounter are extremely remote, but why take a chance? With a can of pepper spray on your hip, you need not fear either black bear or grizzly, mountain lion or cow moose. Nights spent around the campfire are no longer unsettling because of the security furnished by that canister of pepper spray.

Species Description

The mountain lion is America's largest unspotted cat, second in size only to the jaguar. A mature adult male weighs about 170–200 pounds, while females weigh about 120 pounds. Its color is tawny and its body is built long (about 8 feet from tip of nose to tip of tail) and low to the ground because of its short legs, which helps it to stay undetected when stalking prey. Its tail is about 3 feet long, with a black tip; the head is smallish with small rounded ears and large yellowish eyes.

Because the mountain lion is secretive and rarely seen by humans, pug marks are often the only evidence left behind to prove that a lion has passed through. A lion's paws are large, about 4 inches long and 4½ inches wide, but not large enough to keep it from sinking into deep snow. Lion tracks are easy to identify because they resemble a house cat's paw print, only much larger. Many times I've hiked along a secluded snow-covered trail in winter, and upon my return discovered fresh lion tracks in my boot prints, left there by a curious individual that followed me for a short distance before moving off.

A mountain lion is generally not vocal, preferring to keep its location secret. However, at times a lion emits a very loud scream—in mating season to make a potential mate aware of its presence, and at other times to warn other lions they are infringing on its territory, though lions also sometimes scream in frustration or exuberance. Contrary to popular belief, a lion's scream does not sound like a hysterical woman, nor is it high-pitched. The lion screams that I've heard have been more of a loud, hoarse, "O-O-O-W!"

Habitat

Lions live wherever their prey lives, but their secretive nature keeps them in cover during daylight hours, and they emerge into open forest only when hunting at night. So secretive is the lion that many people who live in lion country are not aware that lions live among them. Several people who live in rural homes have related stories to me about wandering into the scrub just beyond their backyard and finding where a lion had killed a deer. Until that moment, they had no idea mountain lions lived nearby.

Range and Population

The mountain lion ranges from the very northern tip of the Rockies in British Columbia down through the entire Rocky Mountains and into Mexico, where it shares its range with an even larger cat, the jaguar. I've been amazed to find lions living at the very pinnacles of the Rockies. The lion is an excellent climber and has no trouble navigating steep, rocky cliffs while stalking bighorn sheep. And in the foothills of the Rockies, where dense sagebrush and oak brush infest the land, the lion is at home and actually prefers these dense tangles that harbor a plentiful supply of large prey animals ranging from javelina to mule deer and elk.

Lion populations throughout the Rocky Mountain states are booming. Areas where lions had not been seen in decades now have lions roaming there. A 1970 population estimate of lions in the Rocky Mountain states put the number at about 5,000. Today, that number has skyrocketed to 25,000, due mainly to aggressive lion conservation efforts by western states, which includes very limited lion hunting and a more tolerant attitude by westerners toward the big cat.

Mating

A female lion may come into heat at any month of the year. Kittens have been observed in the dead of winter, proof that a female came into heat sometime in fall. This is an unfortunate occurrence because the small lions usually succumb to the elements. Fortunately, most female lions come into heat in late February. During this time males roam extensively in search of receptive females, and furious battles—often to the death—occur between mature males. When a male finds a female in heat, he stays with her for about ten days and mates her numerous times before moving off to find another female in heat.

After about three months, the female gives birth to two to four spotted kittens, which are sightless at birth. This is a very difficult time for both kittens and mother. The mother must occasionally leave her young to hunt, and during this time the kittens often wander into the open, where other predators, including other lions, prey on them. For this reason the female urges the kittens to accompany her on her hunts, not only to keep them safe, but also to teach them how to hunt.

Young cats grow fast, and by late fall weigh about forty pounds and are big enough to hunt small and medium-sized prey animals on their own. During this time the female weans her offspring by cuffing and biting them and chasing them away.

THE LYNX

L ife for the lynx is precarious and oftentimes beyond its control, its existence being dictated instead by the presence, or absence, of a gaunt, lightning quick rodent called the snowshoe hare. A lynx may occasionally take a wayward ptarmigan or careless red squirrel, but the speedy hare comprises 95 percent of its diet.

The lynx is an excellent hunter, but sometimes that's not enough because the snowshoe hare population exists in a boom and bust cycle of roughly ten years. During the midpoint of this cycle, when hare numbers are healthy, the lynx population is also healthy and increases as the hare increases. If lynx numbers are sufficient to keep the hares in check, catastrophic overpopulation can be postponed. In areas where the lynx is not prevalent, the hare's peak cycle occurs every seven years, but where the lynx population is healthy, the peak cycle is set back to every ten years.

Unfortunately, a major die-off of hares is inevitable, regardless of predation. A female snowshoe hare produces three to four litters of eight per year; and soon the offspring produce offspring, and on and on, resulting in an exponential rise in hare numbers. Eventually, even a burgeoning lynx community fails to keep hares in check and gross overpopulation results. At the peak of the hare's cycle, it is not unusual to count 2,000 per square mile. Then starvation and disease wipes out the population in a matter of weeks and leaves the forest devoid of hares. This sudden die-off leaves the burgeoning lynx population with virtually no prey base overnight, and ultimately leads to slow, torturous deaths from starvation. The relationship between the lynx and snowshoe hare remains the essence of codependence between predator and prey. Both species need each other to avoid catastrophe.

Perfect Prey Versus Perfect Predator

Mother Nature has equipped the snowshoe hare with the perfect tools to escape almost any predator. Its body is long and slim for racing; its over-size rear paws have dense tufts of fur between the toes which serve as snowshoes. While other predators, such as the wolf or wolverine, flounder in the deep, powdery snow, the hare races effortlessly across these expanses and makes a mockery of any race.

If that wasn't enough, the snowshoe hare, also called the varying hare, grows an overcoat of pure white guard hairs in fall that hides its dusty brown summer coat and makes the hare almost invisible while sitting among branches in the snow. Only a coal-black nose and ear tips break the dazzling white camouflage. In spring, the white guard hairs shed and the hare's brown undercoat remains, and again the animal is camouflaged against its surroundings.

It would seem that nature has tipped the odds totally in the hare's favor. But nature has also provided the lynx with very special gifts for the formidable task of pursuing the speedy snowshoe hare. A mature lynx has an elongated body built for speed, much like a greyhound's, with long legs and oversized paws. And nature did not quit here. Growing between the toes on each paw are dense tufts of fur that also act as snowshoes. When the hare takes off across the soft snow like a furry white rocket, the lynx is able not only to pursue it, but to gain ground.

Prime snowshoe-hare habitat is a young forest about five to fifty years after a fire, where dense thickets of young trees and brush such as willow and alder flourish and provide plenty of bark for food. Unable to spot its prey at a distance, a lynx weaves in and out of thickets, averaging about 2 miles per night of zigzag hunting, though the actual hunting area may be ten acres or less. Normally, the ever-vigilant snowshoe hare would be able to detect the vibration as the larger lynx trundles through the snow nearby and would be long gone before the lynx was even aware of it— except for one more miracle of Mother Nature. In her wisdom, she equipped the lynx's ear tips with long tufts of fur. These act as antennae to pinpoint a snowshoe hare's body tremors from as far away as 40 feet.

When the lynx senses a vibration ahead, it slows to an almost imperceptible stalk. Its eyesight, six times better than a human's, scans the area where the vibrations are coming from until it spots a tuft of fur, or the black nose of a snowshoe hare that is totally unaware of the lynx's presence only 20 feet away. The chase is always short, 40 feet or less; anything longer and the snowshoe will easily dodge its way to safety through dense tangles where not even the lynx can follow.

Much can go wrong during the hunt, and often it does. A hare may see or sense the lynx before it is ready to pounce, or dive into a thicket ahead of the cat. Researchers have found that a lynx averages three kills for every ten hunts and makes a kill about every other day when hare numbers are stable. That's a lot of energy exerted, and since cats possess undersized hearts, the lynx is forced to rest for a half hour before it is strong enough to take up another hunt.

It occurs to me as I study a particular set of snowshoe-hare tracks galloping across the snow—then intercepted by saucer-sized lynx tracks—that

Mother Nature has decided that the lynx and the snowshoe hare are to be left to each other for their sustenance, so specialized has she equipped this predator and prey.

In the frozen north country of Canada and Alaska, another predator joins the dance of death in the snowshoe thickets—man. Indian and white subsistence trappers who live in the backcountry still penetrate the dense forests in search of the lustrous fur of the lynx. In good years, when hares are plentiful, trappers catch upwards of one hundred lynx on their wilderness traplines, which may cover 50 miles or more.

When hare numbers are down and the lynx is scarce, trappers struggle to provide for their families with catches of only a dozen lynx. It's as though Mother Nature requires a strict code of honor for anyone interjecting themselves into this very special predator/prey cycle: a feast for all when the snowshoe hare is plentiful and a desperate struggle to survive when the white rodent disappears. Truly, this is one of the purest examples of the cycle of nature, with man simply another predator.

A Rare Lynx Encounter

The chances of spotting a lynx in its forested habitat are slim, mainly because the snowshoe hare is nocturnal and the lynx does most of its hunting in twilight, and beds down during daylight hours. The only time a traveler is apt to see a lynx is when it is traveling through open country between hunting areas. Studies of radio-collared lynx have shown they have very specific "favorite hunting grounds" where hare concentrations are highest. One lynx spent four weeks in a small forested area no larger than twenty acres, then overnight moved 4 miles to the opposite side of the mountain to another dense thicket of dog-hair cedar below a canopy of spruce trees. The lynx stayed there for three weeks before abruptly moving 2 miles to a dense willow thicket beside a stream. These long stays and abrupt moves indicated the lynx was targeting specific areas it knew from previous successful hunts.

I saw my first lynx in late afternoon while photographing grizzly bears in Glacier National Park on the north side of Huckleberry Mountain. I'd spent the morning hours glassing huckleberry patches located at the very edge of the alpine habitat and had seen two grizzlies. Below my position was a dense spruce and cedar forest, isolated on both sides by several bare areas where massive avalanches had scoured the mountainside a few years before. While I relaxed in the autumn sun, I spotted an animal emerging from a finger of timber a half mile away.

When I brought up my binoculars, my heart raced as I watched a large, silver-furred lynx coming directly at me. I'd hiked up through that avalanche chute at first light, and knew it held ruffed and spruce grouse, but the lynx never slowed to hunt them. Instead, it advanced in its curious, long-legged trot and made a beeline for the dense forest below. The lynx appeared nervous and tense as it moved across the open terrain, and it was only when it neared the security of the forest that it slowed to a walk and finally stopped 10 yards from cover. The lynx paused for a few seconds to survey its back trail. Then, with a flick of the tail, it melted into the dense cedar forest.

I've seen two other lynx, one in Canada's Banff National Park, the other in the North Fork Flathead River country of western Montana. Each sighting was typical—the lynx appeared to be nervous and in a hurry while crossing open country and moved in a steady, purposeful gait on its way to another secluded hunting ground. I've never heard of anyone spying a lynx lying along a gurgling stream while watching trout in a pool, or sitting patiently in a meadow waiting for a juicy mouse to scurry by. That's just not lynxlike. This predator's security and sustenance lies in the tangles of those high country forests way back in the wilderness, where man rarely ventures, and where the lynx and the snowshoe hare nightly play out their bittersweet dance of life and death.

Danger Stalks the Roaming Lynx

A lynx is rarely found more than 100 feet away from a tree, and for good reason. Researchers following radio-collared lynx in one instance found where the animal had been surprised in an alpine meadow by a pack of wolves. The nearest tree was 100 yards away, and the wolves killed and ate the lynx before it could make it to the safety of the tree. And even if a lynx climbs a tree, it's low enough on the food chain that larger tree-climbing predators sometimes prey on it. The same researchers found where another lynx had climbed a tree to escape a mountain lion, but the big cat followed it up the tree and killed it.

Most lynx sightings occur during the first few years after the snow-shoe population crashes. Robbed of its favorite prey, the lynx must wander beyond the security of dense forest if it is to survive. This long-legged cat has been known to travel 50 miles or more seeking the snowshoe hare or other suitable prey. One lynx even traveled from Great Slave Lake in Northwest Territories to Edmonton, Alberta, a distance of almost 700 miles!

During this period of desperate wandering, a mature lynx is most likely to attack larger prey. In Alaska that may be a caribou or Dall sheep; in Canada, a white-tailed deer or caribou; and in the lower states, a white-tail or mule deer. An Alaskan wildlife biologist who investigated a caribou killed by a lynx stated, "From the sign in the snow, it was a long, drawn-out affair. The lynx jumped on the caribou's back and rode it for 300 yards while it chewed and bit at its neck. The carcass looked like a pin cushion from the lynx's claws."

A dozen years ago, I found a yearling white-tailed deer that had been killed by a lynx on the ice of the upper St. Joe River in North Idaho. This is deep snow country, and most deer and elk migrate down slope to brush fields. Each winter, a few deer are slow to leave the high country before deep snow hampers their escape. These animals eke out a meager existence nibbling on brush along the river, and some die from starvation. This particular deer may have been too weak to escape, but the signs on the ice indicated a struggle, and the many lynx tracks around the carcass indicated that the lynx had indeed killed the deer.

During that first, devastating winter when the snowshoe cycle busts, the normally reclusive lynx has even been seen roaming along rural plowed roads, or lurking near backcountry towns or ranches, where the scent of livestock or the presence of mice or barn rats draws in this reluctant wilderness dweller. It's also a death sentence because lynx fur has always brought a high price.

Hudson Bay Pursues the Lynx

Lynx fur is soft and lustrous and has always been a favorite of the fur trade. From the earliest days of colonization in Canada, the lynx has been pursued by trappers. Hudson Bay Trading Company established remote fur trading posts throughout Canada and the northern border states to take in tens of millions of animal pelts.

Depending on the fickle fashion tastes of Europe, certain furs were in demand and fetched higher prices, which meant thousands of trappers pursued that species. The beaver, for example, was in great demand for about twenty years beginning in the 1830s. Its fur is not considered very attractive, being shaggy and coarse, but the undercoat is dense and lustrous. Furriers sheared away the coarse long hair and dyed the under-fur for use in making men's top hats. As a result the beaver was almost wiped out of the streams north and south of the border, until silk top hats came into fashion.

Lynx fur, however, was always in demand, and trappers exacted a heavy toll. During the upper half of the snowshoe-hare cycle, when lynx were abundant, Hudson Bay took in anywhere from 50,000 to 80,000 pelts annually. This cycle continued until 1930, when high prices for lynx pelts sent greedy trappers after the cat during the low point of the snowshoe-hare cycle. Though fewer than 1,000 pelts were brought in that winter, they represented the seed crop, and the lynx has never fully recovered.

One curious problem of the Hudson Bay era was that the higher-priced lynx pelt was often confused with the similar, but lower-priced bobcat. Trappers and fur buyers often claimed a spotted bobcat pelt was a lynx and began calling them lynx cats. To avoid confusion, Hudson Bay officials countered with the label of "Canadian lynx," for any real thing. That terminology stuck, and has even become integrated into academic circles, where the scientific classification for the lynx is *Lynx canadensis.* Today, most knowledgeable cat people refer to the lynx as "Canadian lynx."

Lynx Attacks on Humans Are Rare

Attacks on humans are rare. A lynx is simply not large enough to tackle something as large as a human. A Canadian trapper was trudging home on a bitter cold winter evening with twelve snowshoe hares slung over his back when a lynx sneaked up behind him and jumped onto his back. The startled trapper managed to strangle the lynx. Obviously, the snowshoe hare was in abundance, but this lynx may have had an injury that slowed it down enough that it couldn't catch the speedy animals.

Another attack occurred as a man wearing a buckskin coat snow-shoed through deep snow during a blizzard, and a lynx jumped from a limb above onto his back. When the man yelled, the lynx bounded off. No doubt, the lynx had thought the man was a deer.

A Murder in Lynx Country

Western Montana and northern Idaho are at the southern tip of lynx country. In these environs the lynx's hold is precarious, and every animal taken out of the ecosystem has the potential to cause irreparable harm. In the summer of 1971, I was privy to a lynx murder that haunts me to this day.

I was working in the St. Joe National Forest as a construction inspector on the Gold Creek Road, which cut through the heart of wilderness along the state line between Idaho and Montana. It was a wonderful job for a nature lover like me, and I spent many hours searching for wolverine, wolf, lynx and grizzly bear sign, to the point where other Forest Service employees chided me as being born a hundred years too late.

The road was built to a rough grade, and the next chore was to install drainage culverts. The crew for this consisted of a foreman and four laborers—all tough men who were always shooting their rifles at various targets, some as innocuous as a tin can, but other times it was a snowshoe hare or a red squirrel.

I learned from another worker that one of the men on the culvert crew had shot a large black bear because the foreman wanted a bear-skin rug. Bear season was closed, and it was also illegal to shoot another man's game animal. But in those days, bears were considered pests, and many men shot them on sight. Being new to the country and my job, I said nothing.

A few weeks later, a fellow Forest Service inspector asked me, "Did you hear about the guys on the culvert crew shooting a lynx?"

The incident, I learned, began while the men were taking a mid-morning break. One of the guys looked up and saw a long-legged cat walking along the road's shoulder 200 yards away. He hurried to his pickup and returned with a rifle and looked at the animal through the rifle's scope. He excitedly informed his cohorts that it was a lynx. Egged on by crew members, the man took a steady aim by laying the rifle across the hood of his pickup. As the shot rang out, the lynx jumped high into the air and was dead when it hit the ground.

I was somewhat skeptical that the animal they'd shot was a lynx, so the other inspector and I drove down to the area where the animal reportedly had been shot. We spotted fur in the brush below the road and skidded down the steep slope to investigate. My heart sank as I stared into the glazed eyes of the dead lynx, a twenty-five-pound female. I felt anger and shame: anger at the cruel men who had so wantonly murdered such a delicate, precious animal; and shame that I had not confronted them after they'd shot the black bear. Maybe I could have put some fear into them by threatening to have them arrested or complained to their supervisor and requested there be no shooting on the job site.

I called the game warden and he investigated the lynx shooting, but the entire culvert crew played dumb and escaped punishment. Through the years the implications of this senseless act of murder by men with no morals or conscience has haunted me when I struggle to find a viable breeding population of lynx in this area, which is my home range. Had this removal of a breeding-age female from the ecosystem so many years ago doomed a struggling lynx population? Call me overly dramatic, but I've learned that most environmental calamities are caused by men who do stupid things, and by those who stand by and say nothing.

Species Description

A mature male lynx weighs about thirty pounds, and a female tops out at about twenty-five pounds. However, a lynx looks much larger because of its elongated, greyhoundlike body with long legs and its heavy coat of fluffy, light gray fur. A lynx is sometimes mistaken for its near relative, the bobcat, because both species are similar in size and appearance. The best way to differentiate these cats is by leg length. A bobcat's legs are in proportion with its body, while a lynx's legs are stiltlike and its gait more of a stiff trot than a walk. In addition a lynx's ear tufts are much longer than those of a bobcat.

A lynx's paws, as mentioned previously, are oversized and act as snowshoes to keep it from sinking into deep snow. At 4 inches across, the lynx's paw print is about the same size of a mountain lion's. The best way to tell the difference between a lynx track and a lion track is to examine the toes. A lion's four toes will be prominent in its pug mark, while a lynx's track will show small toe print spread out in its pug mark. A bobcat's track is much smaller than a lynx's track and is in proportion with its body.

Habitat

Lynx rarely venture into the low country because their main food source, the snowshoe hare, is found primarily in higher elevations where deep snows provide much water to allow alder and willow brush to flourish. Lynx do not prefer any environment, such as mature forest. Instead, a lynx seeks any habitat where the snowshoe is found, and that is usually dense tangles of brush or high-country cedar swamps.

My favorite time to slip through these high-country hare havens is in midwinter, when several feet of snow lie upon the land, and trees crack from the intense cold. It is here that I find a plethora of snowshoe-hare tracks and droppings, and an occasional enormously wide lynx track, as I meander around thickets too dense to navigate with my rawhide-webbed snowshoes. Eventually, I'll spot a flash of white fur—gone in the blink of an eye—leaving me to wonder how a lynx could possibly make its living catching these furry white blurs.

Range and Population

Lynx are found throughout the Canadian Rockies, with a population estimated at about 200,000. Again, lynx range and distribution is a perfect overlay of snowshoe hare range. Alaska's lynx numbers are about 150,000. But when dense forests give way to treeless tundra, lynx numbers quickly fade, even though the arctic hare is in abundance. Without trees for escape, the lynx can't survive predation by wolves.

South of the Canadian border, lynx numbers thin out dramatically. About 300 lynx live just south of the border in western Montana. North Idaho has about 200 lynx. They are also occasionally sighted in northeast Washington. Yellowstone National Park also holds about 50 lynx. Colorado has recently begun a lynx transplant program. Animals supplied by Canadian trappers have been released in the northwestern corner of the state near Rocky Mountain National Park, where a healthy snowshoe population exists. Curiously, these areas, which represent the southern tip of the snowshoe hare's range, do not experience the ten-year boom-and-bust cycle.

The Rocky Mountains to the south hold scant, if any, snowshoe hares. Though several other prey animals exist, such as the cottontail rabbit and jackrabbit, the lynx is absent from these ecosystems because the lynx possesses specific predatory skills, all tied to its pursuit of the snowshoe hare.

Mating

Female lynx are capable of mating at one year of age and come into heat in March. When a male lynx finds a receptive female, he stays with her for about a week, mating her numerous times during this period, then moves off when the female is no longer in heat. There is no strong family tie between male and female. In fact male lynx have been known to kill and eat kittens.

The female makes a den under a log or overturned trees roots, and after a gestation period of about sixty days, three or four kittens are born. These kits have a downy coat of brown with black spots, and are sightless for about ten days after birth. Within weeks the kittens are able to hunt for mice and voles around the den, and are soon accompanying the female on hunts for snowshoe hares, thereby learning how to hunt this dietary staple and where the best hunting grounds are found. This family often unit stays together all winter, with mother and young hunting the same hare thickets. When mating season begins in March, the family unit disperses.

Bobcat

THE BOBCAT

The bobcat lay in wait behind a boulder at the mouth of a small cave in northern New Mexico's San Juan Mountains. With the setting of the sun came the sudden flutter of wings from within. The bobcat tensed. A second later a pallid bat shot out. The cat sprang into the air, but the bat dodged its flailing paws.

The bobcat quickly returned to its hiding place and bunched its legs for the next leap. Another bat whizzed out of the cave, but this time the bobcat leaped into the air and, using lightning-quick reflexes, swatted the dodging bat to the rocky ground. Before the fluttering mammal could become airborne, the bobcat pounced on it and shook it violently until the bat went limp. Four ounces of prey were quickly devoured before the bobcat returned to the hunt. Six more bats were caught from among the hundreds that fluttered out of the cave before the bobcat's belly was full.

The Opportunistic Hunter

The bobcat is one of the most opportunistic predators in the Rocky Mountains. Nature has blessed the bobcat with the ability to hunt a variety of small to medium-sized prey animals that competing predators can't hunt successfully. It's surely the only predator that preys on bats!

In the southwestern Rockies, the bobcat's prey may be large vampire bats or rabbits. In the central Rockies, it pursues rabbits and squirrels, and in the northern Rockies, it competes with the lynx for snowshoe hares and red squirrels. When these common prey animals are not available, the bobcat easily switches to alternative prey.

But during lean times, when alternative prey is also in short supply and competing predators roam the land with bellies grumbling, the bobcat sits at the mouth of a bat cave, or uses its lightning-quick reflexes to kill a snake. So varied is the bobcat's prey base, and so accomplished are its hunting abilities, that it seldom faces the prospect of starvation.

A bobcat lacks the initial lightning quickness of the lynx. Neither does it possess the streaking long-distance speed of the mountain coyote, nor the size and power of the mountain lion. But nature has endowed the bobcat with enough speed and size and agility to catch most of the prey these other animals specialize in.

The main diet of bobcats is mice and rats, most of which are found in rock crevices. Find a jumble of rocks in bobcat country, and you can be assured that sooner or later the resident bobcat will be hunting there. Whenever I see a prominent rock outcrop or rock pile, I usually detour over to it and almost always find evidence of a bobcat. Sometimes it's a few tiny rodent bones, or some cat hair left behind from its ambush point behind a boulder. In winter these rocky areas always have cat tracks around them. Most cats begin a very slow stalk when they get within 20 feet of a rocky area to avoid alerting any rodents with their footsteps. So slow is its movement that it is almost imperceptible.

The bobcat's close cousin, the lynx, is endowed with long, pointed ear tufts that act as antennae, picking up snowshoe-hare body vibrations from up to 30 feet away. The bobcat's shorter ear tufts are inferior to the lynx's, but they also serve the same purpose, especially when the bobcat is nosing around rocky areas or log jams. At 10 feet, its antennae sense the vibration of a mouse or pack rat, giving it the advantage during this deadly game of cat and mouse. When all other prey animals are in short supply or nonexistent, a bobcat can count on nabbing a few mice or a juicy pack rat from a rock jumble each day.

Medium-sized rodents, such as rabbits and beaver, are fair game for a bobcat. In the southern Rockies, cottontails and jackrabbits, are favorite prey because they are large enough to furnish food for up to three days. In the central and northern Rockies, the snowshoe hare is on the menu. Though the bobcat lacks the very specific physical abilities of the lynx to catch the elusive snowshoe hare in its dense thickets, the bobcat finds success by hunting hares along the forest fringes, or in the more open lodgepole pine forests, where hares sometimes live.

Bobcats also take a variety of small birds, grouse and ducks—even geese when they migrate through the Rockies. However, birds are never plentiful enough, or, more importantly, site-specific enough—meaning the bobcat doesn't have a particular thicket or rock pile, as with rats and mice, to concentrate its hunt. Most birds are taken by a bobcat as it moves through its hunting areas looking for site-specific prey.

Big Bobcats Hunt Big Prey

Male bobcats occasionally grow much larger than the twenty- to thirty-pound average. I've seen big males that had to weigh forty pounds or more. (I've never heard of a female weighing more than thirty pounds.) Forty-pound specimens in the northern Rockies are not unusual. I viewed one specimen, caught by a trapper, that tipped the scales at forty-eight pounds. When a bobcat gets to about thirty pounds, it loses some of its speed and dexterity to catch mice and small birds, but this added weight and strength allows these bigger cats to hunt larger game, such as mature beavers, smaller deer, and calf elk. Researchers followed one forty-two-pound, radio-collared bobcat that routinely killed thirty-pound beavers, and in one winter killed eight white-tailed deer. This transition from mouse killer to deer killer creates even bigger bobcats because the large quantity of meat and less energy expended from deer hunting often prompts a large bobcat to grow even larger.

When elk calves are still small and feeble, a large bobcat will prey on them. But it must be careful because the 600-pound mother elk is very protective and will stomp the cat. Bobcats weighing thirty pounds or more will also prey upon smaller bighorn sheep, especially lambs and smaller ewes.

Bobcats in the southern Rockies usually don't grow to forty pounds, but some males do surpass thirty pounds. These larger cats are capable of killing small and medium-sized javelina and coati mundi, a neotropical animal that looks like a cross between an anteater and a raccoon.

Beaver: Favorite Prey of the Bobcat

All predators desire beaver meat, which is dark and rich in protein. The muscle fiber exudes the sweet, musky odor of castor oil, which is attractive to every predator from the bobcat to the grizzly bear. Among experienced woodsmen, beaver meat is called "bobcat candy." However, this is a misconception, borne of the fact that bobcats frequently lurk along the fringes of a beaver dam. Sure, a bobcat will take a careless beaver, but most of the bobcat's focus is on the plethora of other prey animals and birds drawn to the secluded, food-rich biome of the beaver pond.

A mature beaver, weighing thirty to fifty pounds and possessing 2-inch-long chisel teeth powerful enough to chew through a tree, is a formidable opponent for a twenty-five-pound bobcat. However, baby beavers, called kits, as well as medium-sized beavers in the ten- to twenty-pound range are preyed upon regularly by bobcats when they leave the safety of the pond and waddle ashore to cut brush or small trees. Even these smaller beavers become dangerous unless the bobcat strikes quickly. Most bobcats kill beavers by pouncing on them and killing them instantly with a bite to the back of the neck. If that fails, the beaver usually escapes by making a bull-like rush for the safety of the pond.

Making a Bobcat Video

One of the most enjoyable outdoor jobs I've had was as a cameraman and on-screen host for Stoney-Wolf Video, makers of high-quality outdoor and nature programs. One year we produced a video entitled, "The Fascinating World of Wildcats." I filmed much of this program, and one segment revolved around two bobcats hunting at a beaver pond in winter.

I'd learned from a landowner that two medium-sized bobcats were hunting daily at a beaver pond in a shallow draw a mile away from his house.

The first day, I arrived in the predawn darkness and set up a portable blind to conceal myself and the big black camera and tripod. I was barely settled when a male bobcat appeared on a downed aspen log and tiptoed across the ice, scanning the pond for beavers or ducks. Out of the corner of my eye I spotted movement, and a second later another bobcat trotted across the ice of a smaller pond with a red squirrel in its mouth. Over the next few days I filmed these two bobcats, no doubt siblings from a spring litter, catching muskrats, mice, and ducks at this pond, but no beavers.

The adult male and female beavers were wary, and the bobcats were not able to get close enough to them the first few days. Then a blizzard blasted the area, dropping snow and temperatures. When the weather cleared I again set up at the beaver pond, which now had a shelf of ice extending halfway across the main pool. Two hours later a bobcat emerged from the brush on the opposite side of the pond and shook the snow from its coat. It gingerly tested the ice before venturing onto it.

Suddenly, the cat froze, then scurried behind a log and crouched. One of the beavers swam about 20 feet away. The cat watched the beaver intently, its feet bunched. Finally, the beaver nosed up to the edge of the ice, climbed onto it and started spreading liquid castor from a gland at the base of its tail over its fur to waterproof it.

The young bobcat crept forward, but hesitated when the ice cracked. No doubt some of the cat's reluctance stemmed from the fact that this beaver was large. Finally, the temptation of the beaver preening with its back turned, just 15 feet away, proved too much. The cat crept forward and made a half-hearted lunge. The instant the bobcat's paw touched it, the big beaver threw itself high into the air and made a back flip that would have made Greg Louganis proud.

The beaver hit the water with a tremendous splash and slapped its tail as it dove, leaving the bobcat alone and frustrated on the ice shelf. The bobcat prowled back and forth, and crouched when the beaver surfaced to tread water less than 5 feet away. In this situation, a mature bobcat probably wouldn't have been able to overpower that beaver because it was so large and had been sitting on the ice right at the edge of deep water.

Bobcat Mortality

A bobcat has many potential predators, but few that routinely prey upon it. A wolf or mountain lion occasionally will catch a bobcat in an open area and kill it, but most cats zip up a tree at the first hint of danger. Of course with the mountain lion that's not always a ticket to safety. Lion hunter Larry Bennet told me that he was driving down a snow-covered forest road at dawn when he cut a fresh mountain lion track crossing the road into a wide creek bottom. Larry released his three lion dogs, and they galloped after the track.

Expecting the usual long and arduous chase, Larry was surprised to hear the hounds baying "treed" barely a minute later. He arrived at the base of a limby Douglas fir and quickly tied up his dogs. He looked up and was confounded to see a large bobcat precariously perched at the end of a limb 40 feet above. At first he thought his dogs had detoured from the lion track when they cut the bobcat's scent. Then he heard claws scraping on bark and was startled to see a ninety-pound female lion glaring down at him from a limb below the bobcat. Larry told me, "I'm sure I interrupted that lion hunt. I backtracked and saw where she'd cut the bobcat track and followed it and chased it up the tree just before I let the dogs loose."

Humans take a toll on bobcats during the winter months when deep snow forces the cats down to lower elevations near roads. Lion hunters chase them, and trappers use beaver bait to lure bobcats into traps. Normally, the mortality is not too great because there are not too many cat hunters or trappers anymore due to lower fur prices. However, when fur prices rise, humans often take a fearful toll.

In the early 1990s bobcat hides were much desired by European furriers, who used the cat's white and black spotted belly fur to make coats for the rich. Prices skyrocketed to $400 to $500 for a bobcat pelt, and many people took to the woods with grandpa's old traps to pursue an easy paycheck trapping bobcats. Few of these people knew what they were doing, and instead trapped many other animals and birds unintentionally. One time I found a dead horse with eight rusted old traps set around it. The trapper, I learned, had taken an old horse that a neighbor wanted to be put down into the woods and shot it, then used it for bait.

The above effort seems ludicrous. Unfortunately, bobcats are not trap-shy and come in readily to any kind of bait, even when the traps are in plain view. Two bobcats were trapped at that horse carcass. During this period of high fur prices, many drainages in the West lost entire bobcat populations. One large drainage near my Montana home that normally held about fifteen bobcats, had its population wiped out. It took several years after fur prices dropped before cats from more remote areas moved in.

Fortunately, the Rocky Mountains have many remote, rugged areas, even in the Southwest, where snow depths remain low all winter. The bobcat prospers in these backcountry haunts, which provide surplus animals to replace cats that die from fights or predation. You may never see a bobcat, even in prime cat country, but rest assured, this silent hunter is somewhere out there stalking a plump rodent.

Species Description

From a distance, it is difficult to tell a bobcat from a lynx, so similar are these two predators. However, a bobcat does not possess the long, stiltlike legs and stiff, trotting gait of the lynx. Its pace instead resembles a stalking motion, even when it is not hunting. A bobcat's face is also lynxlike, though the twin beards of fur hanging down from its cheeks are not as long as those of the lynx, and its pointed ear tufts are shorter. Also, a bobcat's paws are more in proportion with its body, as opposed to those of a lynx, which are oversized.

A bobcat's coat varies in color from pale gray in open Montana forests, to dusky gray in Idaho brush, to reddish gray in the red rock canyons of the southern Rockies. These color variations help the bobcat blend into its environment in these various habitats. Bobcats have white belly fur with black spots. And, of course, the bobcat has a bobbed, 2-inch-long tail.

Mature male bobcats often weigh thirty-five pounds or more, and an occasional male will tip the scales at forty-five pounds. Females usually weigh no more than twenty-five pounds.

Habitat

Though bobcats are numerous in the Rockies, few people ever see them because they are nocturnal hunters who prefer dense cover. In the southern Rockies that may be thick cactus forest or brush-choked arroyos. In the central Rockies it's oak brush and aspen thickets, and in the northern Rockies it is tangled stream bottoms and dark forests.

Some bobcats find good hunting in the higher country near timberline in areas more suitable for the Canadian lynx. These individuals hunt snowshoe hares along the fringes of swampy thickets and supplement their diets with ptarmigan and grouse. They also hunt the pica, a smallish rodent that looks like a cross between a pack rat and a rabbit and lives in rocky areas. However, a bobcat's paws are not oversized like those of a lynx, so when snow begins to build up in the high country the bobcat is forced to migrate down slope.

I had an interesting experience with a bobcat one winter when I lived in a small Montana cabin in the high country 7 miles from the Idaho border. This is heavily forested deep-snow country, with 8 feet of snow the norm. In early November a heavy snowstorm stranded deer and elk, along with predators, many of which slowly starved to death over the winter.

On a mid-December morning I went outside to shovel 8 inches of snow that had fallen overnight on the existing 4 feet of white stuff. To my surprise, a set of bobcat tracks led from under my front porch to a wood shed beside the garage. I strapped on a pair of snowshoes and followed the tracks as the bobcat floundered through the powdery snow to a seasonal cabin 200 yards away. The cabin's eaves sheltered the base of the building from snow, and even showed some bare ground. The cat's tracks slid down into this narrow crease alongside the building and emerged again into the snow from under the front porch. I followed the tracks from cabin to cabin for two hours, but never did see the cat making them.

Throughout the winter, storm after storm buried the land deeper under a suffocating blanket of snow. The enterprising bobcat made its rounds about every other day to the cabins and other structures, where it hunted field mice and pack rats. These rodents often invade dwellings to escape the snow and become a problem as the winter wears on. I got into the habit of leaving the door up on my garage, which allowed the bobcat to sneak in and help me rid that structure of rodent pests.

Range and Population

Most predators have a very loosely defined home range where they roam at random while hunting. A bobcat's range, however, is well-defined. Most bobcats have a home range of about 2 square miles, which they identify with claw marks on trees and urine scent posts at strategic places. This marking is not only to makes the opposite sex aware that they are available, but also warns strange cats to stay out of their hunting area.

Within a bobcat's range, it hunts at very specific sites, such as beaver ponds. Its next hunting site may be a rock outcrop on top of a ridge a half-mile away. The bobcat might snoop around downed trees for mice, or pinecone caches for red squirrels as it moves toward the rocky outcrop. These areas may or may not produce a meal, but the rock outcrop continues to be the cat's destination because it knows from many successful hunts it will find opportunities there.

This strict adherence to a site-specific hunting pattern makes the bobcat very predictable. Within its range a bobcat will make the rounds of its favorite hunting areas about every ten to fourteen days. During that time every log jumble, beaver pond, and rock outcrop will be investigated. Even if the hunting is good at a particular rock outcrop and the cat catches two plump half-pound pack rats in an hour, it will not hunt there for the next several days. Instead, it licks its chops and grooms its bloody beard, and continues on toward the next hunting area.

Bobcats are found north of the Canadian border into southern British Columbia, but the cat is not seen farther north because it struggles to get around in the deep snow of these northern latitudes. The bobcat is numerous throughout the Rocky Mountain states south of the Canadian border; its numbers are too great to accurately count, but biologists guess that there may be upwards of 200,000 bobcats roaming the Rockies.

Mating

In late winter, usually March, bobcat breeding season begins. During this time males roam extensively beyond their home range in search of females. Fights between invading and protective males are common, with the bigger forty-pound cats holding a decided edge in battle. Some of these males later die, either directly from fighting, or indirectly, when injuries keep them from hunting efficiently.

An encounter between an amorous male and female bobcat is best described as chaotic. The male pounces on the female, which scratches and bites at the male until she is overpowered. The male climbs onto the female's back and holds her down by biting her neck fur, and then mounts her. All the while the male is growling menacingly and the female is caterwauling unmercifully. Truly a love match made in hell.

When mating is complete, the female shoots out from under the male and never looks back. About six weeks later three to four tiny kittens are born in a den located under a downed tree or small cave. The female keeps her young here until they have opened their eyes, then leaves them to go on short hunts nearby. She brings back live mice and drops them in front of her kittens, at which point instinct takes over and the young bob-cats pounce on the offering. Within weeks, the kittens are hunting mice, chipmunks, and small birds close to the den. I know of no other predator whose young become successful hunters so early in their lives.

The mother bobcat takes the kittens along on her hunts, showing them site-specific hunting methods, but as the kittens grow and become somewhat competitive in the search for food, the female begins to rough them up, until the kittens finally move off on their own. This occurs sometime in September. The kittens may shadow the female for a few months while she hunts, but the pressure of mating season usually disperses these young cats to seek their own home range to hunt.

THE WOLVERINE

Gary Holmes

A t a country gas station in western Montana a few years ago, I noticed a man walking with a curious limp. Upon closer inspection, I noticed that the cowboy boot on his right foot had the top torn away.

When I asked the gentleman about the boot, the man scowled and snapped, "Damn wolverine!" Whereupon I pestered the story out of him.

My newfound friend and his buddy went horseback camping along the Idaho/Montana border at an isolated mountain lake teeming with large cutthroat trout. The men were in bear country, so they cached their food high in a tree a few hundred yards from camp. They then switched from cowboy boots to tennis shoes, inflated a rubber raft and paddled to the far side of the lake to fish. A half hour had gone by when the man glanced back and noticed a smallish animal roaming through their campsite.

At first, both men thought it was a badger, but then the other guy correctly identified it as a wolverine. The men paddled furiously to shore, yelling and waving to chase the pesky critter off. The wolverine stopped nosing their packs, spotted the advancing men and, with a ferocious snarl and fangs bared, charged. The panicked men dove for the safety of their rubber raft.

The wolverine stalked back to the campsite, sat on its haunches and calmly ate the top half of my newfound friend's cowboy boot! The anger rose in the man's voice when he said, "If I coulda got to my gun in camp, I'da showed him who's boss. But no way was I gonna risk my life for a cowboy boot."

The above anecdote is typical of a wolverine encounter. This mysterious animal takes no quarter and gives none; its only desire is to be left alone to be a wolverine. But when disturbed, it becomes a whirling mass of frightening snarls and slashing fangs that doesn't know how to retreat. Unfortunately, such qualities are not appreciated by all who encounter the wolverine, resulting in its rather checkered reputation, which ranges from demon to glutton to thief.

A Fierce Reputation

The hardy French-Canadian trappers of the eighteenth century called the wolverine Le Carcajou, the glutton, while the various Indian tribes had their own names for this animal, though they all generally translated the same: a hard character, evil one, or devil bear. Stories abound of the fearless tenacity and mayhem created by the wolverine. So legendary are its feats that we sometimes lose sight of the fact that we're dealing with a thirty-pound animal.

Beginning with the earliest fur trading expeditions to the New World, woodsmen returned from the wilderness with stories about a demonic beast, smallish in size, but fiendish in its ability to rob the bait and animals from their traplines and steal food stored in cabins. The Indians truly hated the "devil bear" because of its proclivity to dig up and eat the flesh of their ancestors.

Actually, some of the wolverine tales that have drifted down from the Far North are dubious at best, like the one about the polar bear that tangled with a wolverine. As the story goes, the half-ton bear grabbed the little wolverine and squeezed it to its chest, intending to crush it, but the polar bear soon toppled over. The wolverine had torn through the bear's chest and eaten its heart. Hmmm!

Tall tales notwithstanding, enough documented stories exist to give credence to the wolverine's fierceness. One naturalist watched a large male wolverine take over a moose carcass from a 300-pound black bear. The wolverine's loud, vicious snarling and snapping teeth unnerved the bear and it fled. Another northland traveler once watched as a wolverine chased two wolves away from a caribou carcass.

But it would be entirely misleading to say the wolverine backs down from no man or animal. Under normal circumstances, a wolverine will quickly leave an area when it encounters a human. Several years ago I encountered a wolverine on a backcountry trail in Idaho. The wolverine hopped onto a boulder 20 yards away, silently studied me for several seconds, then loped into the huckleberry brush. It is only when protecting its food that a wolverine may refuse to leave when man or beast arrive.

A wolverine backed against a tree is indeed a fierce adversary, but it is by no means invincible; and as it travels through its wilderness home, a wolverine may fall prey to other specialized predators. The notion that a wolverine is ferocious enough to back off a grizzly bear is pure fabrication, unless the bear had a full belly and planned to move on.

I know grizzly bears, and I know wolverines. No animal in the Rocky Mountains could survive the sledgehammer-like swipe from a furious grizzly. I once watched a grizzly kill a black bear with a single blow, and I've seen a grizzly dispatch a cow elk with one bite to its neck. As fierce as it is for its size, a wolverine would be easy prey for the mighty grizzly bear.

Other predators, such as wolves and mountain lions, also prey upon wolverines. Two biologists tracking a radio-collared mountain lion in

British Columbia discovered the lion had twice stalked and killed wolverines. And after watching the deadly efficiency of wolves taking down elk in Yellowstone National Park, I find it difficult to believe that any animal, including the grizzly bear, could withstand the lightning speed and powerful slashing fangs of a half-dozen determined wolves.

That's not to say that a wolverine is too slow and too small to kill prey. On the contrary, Le Carcajou is not above killing prey much larger than itself if the opportunity is presented.

Several documented stories of extraordinary wolverine predation upon 2,000-pound moose have come from the north country. In 1907 near Great Slave Lake, Alberta, observers for the Canadian Geological Survey came upon a three-year-old bull moose floundering and near death in deep snow. After the men shot the moose, they spotted a wolverine loping away. Upon closer inspection, they discovered a huge hole torn into the rear of the hams at the end of the backbone. If they had not interrupted this drama, they felt sure the wolverine would have soon killed the moose.

Eyewitness accounts also attest to the fact that a wolverine is capable of killing a caribou when the opportunity arises. Usually, a wolverine jumps on the neck and then holds on for dear life while frantically tearing at the caribou's throat.

And a few years ago, winter visitors to Glacier National Park were gazing at the breathtaking beauty of McDonald Lake from the lodge when they spotted a whitetail deer limping along the frozen lake 100 yards away. Suddenly a wolverine bounded onto the ice and rapidly overtook the struggling deer. The wolverine jumped onto the animal's neck and quickly killed it.

The Glutton

The wolverine's Latin name, *Gulo gulo,* means "glutton." The earliest records from the founders of Hudson's Bay fur trading posts in the early 1700s mention the wolverine's amazing capacity to consume volumes of food far beyond its smallish size. They tell of thirty-pound wolverines consuming in a single night animal carcasses or valuable stored goods many times their body weight.

We can blame Mother Nature for the wolverine's gluttonous tendencies. Unlike other members of the sleek, lightning-fast weasel family, such as the ermine, fisher, and marten, Mother Nature seems to have shortchanged the wolverine in the natural world, where survival usually goes to the quick. But nature has equipped the wolverine with other unique attributes which allow it to exist when and where other animal species would surely starve.

Because it fails as a supreme predator, the wolverine relies mostly on scavenged food, never in abundance in the wilderness. Many of its quirky habits are a result of its never-ending search for a very limited food supply.

The wolverine roams the lonely avalanche chutes in spring and summer, searching for winter-killed animal carcasses. In winter it drops down to the dense forests, where big game animals congregate and where lions, bears and wolves make kills and leave enough scraps behind to sustain the enterprising wolverine. Much of its diet is a meager menu of a few scraps of hide and the marrow sucked from bones crushed in its powerful jaws—enough to survive, but never enough to satiate its gluttonous appetite.

So sensitive is the wolverine's nose that a single errant molecule of rancid flesh wafting in the breeze is enough to cause the animal to change course and make a beeline for the source. A biologist who live-trapped wolverines for a study in the North Fork Flathead River near Glacier National Park told of finding wolverine tracks in the snow a mile from a live trap baited with a basketball-sized chunk of horse meat.

Even at twenty degrees below zero, enough odor had escaped from the frozen bait to prompt the wolverine to abruptly turn toward the trap. This particular live-trapped wolverine was a twenty-eight-pound male. Though he had been in the trap for only a day, he had almost succeeded in chewing through two 6-inch logs before being sedated, tested, and released.

Wildlife biologists have long marveled at how a forty-pound animal with a stomach as large as a softball could possibly consume hundreds of pounds of food in a single night. That mystery was solved when a naturalist observed a wolverine approaching a freshly killed caribou left behind by Eskimos one morning. That naturalist noted, "I have never seen such a small animal dispose of such a large amount of flesh so quickly. The wolverine immediately pounced on the carcass and began slicing it into football-sized chunks."

Each chunk was then carried off and buried for later use. The trips were short at first, but then the wolverine left for periods up to a half-hour, no doubt storing the meat in more distant hiding places. The naturalist counted sixteen trips that the wolverine made into the brush.

When the Eskimos arrived, they were outraged to discover the carcass almost devoid of meat. Unfortunately, the wolverine refused to abandon the remains of the carcass and met the armed men with fierce snarls and bared fangs, whereupon the Eskimos shot it.

That seems to be the fate of most wolverines who encounter man, and it almost always occurs during the late fall and winter seasons. This is the time when the wolverine drops down to dense forests, where trappers, recreationists, hunters, and fringe human dwellers exact a toll on the glutton—though its only crime is hunger.

Native peoples of the Far North eke out an austere existence by harvesting and drying moose, caribou, and salmon meat in summer and fall. They store this food in small huts, called caches, built atop high stilts. To keep these critical food caches safe from marauding wolverines and bears, sheets of metal are wrapped around the stilts to keep animals from climbing the poles. No matter, a determined wolverine will often chew away at the sheet metal until it can scramble up the slippery poles and gorge on the contents of the cache.

Even food stored behind stout cabin doors is susceptible to a wolverine's rampage. An old Alaskan trapper told me that a decade ago he had packed about 400 pounds of food staples to his main cabin in late fall, then left to pack supplies to another cabin 20 miles away. When he returned two nights later, he discovered a 12-inch-diameter hole chewed through the main cabin's 3-inch-thick front door. Inside, a horrifying mess and stench greeted him, along with the loud snarling of a wolverine protecting its food. The animal made several false charges, and when it became apparent that the "Devil Bear" was not going to leave, the trapper shot it.

The devastation was total. The wolverine had torn open fifty-pound sacks of flour and corn meal, ripped apart bags of sugar and coffee, and had bitten into almost every tin can. What food had not been eaten or packed off the wolverine had sprayed with its putrid, skunklike scent. The trapper was forced to abandon that entire trapline and move south to work as a dishwasher in Anchorage through the winter, so I guess there is some poetic justice to this story.

The wolverine's voracious appetite for food further alienates this taciturn predator's standing with humans when it goes beyond stealing food to stealing livelihoods. In years past, and even today, Indians, Eskimos, and a small number of white men continue to ply the historic trade of running winter traplines for profit and food. In the bitter cold of the snow-covered North, furbearers grow thick, lustrous coats, and these solitary men pursue surplus furbearers as a part of nature's cycle.

Unfortunately, the wolverine is an interloper that looks upon this endeavor with the eyes of an opportunist. A trapline that has taken weeks of hard labor to be laid out may be rendered inoperable in one night when "The Evil One" travels its course, stealing the bait and tearing apart trapped animals.

If Le Carcajou were as stealthy as the cunning wolf, or as solitary as the mighty grizzly, its mayhem would be discovered by frustrated humans long after its departure. But "The Glutton" simply cannot relinquish even leftovers to another, be it animal or human.

This amounts to a death wish for the wolverine because such bravado against the mighty grizzly bear ends quickly with powerful jaws crushing its resistance. Man, on the other hand, sends forth a screaming piece of hot death to extinguish its life. Nevertheless, the wolverine faces this certain doom with a ferocious snarl and bared fangs. Such is the nature of this brave and horrible beast we call the wolverine.

> For Le Carcajou refuses to bend at the knee,
> or retreat or submissively cower and flee.
> And my wish is that one day this urbanized heart
> would swell with fierce courage to set me apart,
> to be filled with the spirit of the wolverine's heart.
>
> —*Mike Lapinski, 2005*

Species Description

A wolverine's body is compact and squat, built for power and endurance, not speed. Males weigh thirty to forty pounds, while females weigh in the twenty- to thirty-pound range. A mature wolverine stands about 16 inches at the shoulder, with long, dark brown fur and two pale, yellowish gray stripes along its shoulder and flanks. Bringing up the rear is a long, bushy tail that often carries the stripe on both sides. Females tend to be a bit darker than males.

A wolverine's paws are disproportionately large and closely resemble in size the track of the much larger mountain lion, except that the wolverine has a fifth toe and a rear heel pad. These oversize paws act as snowshoes and help the wolverine travel over deep snow without floundering.

One of the wolverine's greatest assets is its voice. When alarmed it emits a ferocious, guttural growl. This demonic vocal display of rage is a valuable tool when defending its food cache from larger predators.

The wolverine is the largest member of the weasel family, which also includes the badger, otter, fisher, marten, and ermine (weasel). Interestingly, the skunk is also a member of the weasel family. All are hunters, and all possess a set of wicked set of sharp teeth for killing and tearing flesh. The badger, weighing twenty pounds, somewhat resembles a wolverine with its black masked face and squat build, and is sometimes mistaken for a wolverine.

A few years ago in August, I stopped at the Lookout Pass Ski Area and Resort on the state line between Idaho and Montana. Two hikers informed me that they'd observed a wolverine digging for ground squirrels on the lower part of a ski slope a hundred yards from the main lodge. I thought this odd because a wolverine is normally too shy to forage close to dwellings, and busy Interstate 90 was just a few hundred yards away. I hiked to the area, noticed the mounds of dirt, and then spotted a badger furiously digging at a ground-squirrel burrow.

Habitat

Despite the lines drawn on a map to officially designate an area as wilderness, unless the wolverine roams the land, it remains ecologically suspect. This is because the wolverine, more than any other backcountry dweller, has special needs that allow its survival only in the most remote lands, where flora and fauna exist in natural harmony.

Those other great backcountry dwellers—the lion, the wolf, the grizzly—sometimes have a tendency to roam dangerously close to civilization. In central Idaho's Rockies, wolves sometimes leave the wilderness and get in trouble by dining on an occasional cow or llama. Grizzly bears in fall leave Montana's Bob Marshall Wilderness to invade rural subdivisions to gorge on tasty apples in backyards. And the mountain lion has been known to slip unnoticed into a housing development in the country, whereupon the dogs and cats begin to disappear.

Not the wolverine. You won't hear about a wolverine sneaking into a farmer's chicken coop, or hiding under the front porch. The godly force that created the wolverine has imbued in it a stubborn will and resolute capacity to live in only the most remote pristine habitat of the wilderness.

To find the wolverine you must journey way back to rock bluffs and snowfields, to the very pinnacles of remoteness. These isolated places require so much exertion to get to that humans seldom venture there. Even the dense forests where wolverines occasionally roam tend to be the stunted subalpine variety found at higher elevations just below timberline.

On my summer pilgrimages through the backcountry, I often detour to prime wolverine habitat—that harsh environment in the most desolate alpine reaches where even grass struggles to grow, where snowfields never completely melt between winters. These are, for me, the really fun places to hike because you're so high that the visual splendor of the wildest of the wild is always bouncing off your corneas.

I've seen two wolverines in summer; both were in that band of rugged, remote terrain hidden within the wilderness where few hikers venture. One time while I watched mountain goats frolic above Hidden Lake a mile from the Logan Pass Visitor Center in Glacier National Park, I spotted a set of wide, plodding tracks that crossed a snowfield below the goats. I guessed that they were made by a wolverine because no self-respecting goat would leave the relative security of the rocks to venture across the treacherously steep rotting snow.

Angling toward the tracks, I avoided the dangerous snowfield, reminding myself that a few years back a good friend, Johnny Bauer, had slipped while crossing such a snowfield a few miles away and had fallen to his death.

I circled below to a point where a jumble of huge boulders had collected at the far end of the snowfield. The tracks disappeared into the boulders. It took almost an hour of gingerly picking my way up through twenty-ton rocks before I topped a rise and spotted a well-worn hole in the snow beside a boulder 200 yards away. My binoculars picked up plenty of dirty yellowish hair scattered around the mouth of the hole. I guessed that a wolverine had located a mountain goat carcass, probably killed by a fall or swept off the rocks by an avalanche, and was feeding on the refrigerated carrion. I sat quietly for almost two hours before the lowering sun told the primeval man within that it was time to escape to the cave for the night.

I was excited to have located a wolverine den, but a bit disappointed I hadn't seen the its owner. When I arrived at the main ridge a half-mile away, I looked back and spotted a dark brown wolverine struggling across the snowfield towards the den. I guessed it was a female with a litter of kits somewhere in a rancid cavern near the goat carcass. I luxuriated in the rare sighting, then left the area, lest my presence disturb the mother and cause her to put her kits at risk by moving or abandoning them.

But even the wolverine has limits to what it can endure. In winter these high mountain and alpine zones are constantly buffeted by fierce winds and raging snowstorms, making life impossible for even the hardy wolverine. To escape these conditions the wolverine migrates down to the boreal forest where it scavenges winter-killed big game animals such as elk, moose, and caribou.

This is the midrange belt of wilderness—an area that may hold a few roads or backcountry cabins and is often frequented by horse enthusiasts and hikers in summer—but by the time the wolverine moves down to escape the high country blizzards, 4 feet of snow covers the ground, and it is devoid of human activity except for the hardy fur trapper, home-steader, or snowmobiler. But even with this scant human interaction, it's a dangerous time for the wolverine because humans have food, and this creature knows no boundaries in its search for food.

Range and Population

Historically the wolverine was found throughout the northern forests of America, ranging through the upper Midwest states and east through the seaboard states of New York, Pennsylvania and New England. In the western mountain states, the wolverine ranged all the way down to New Mexico. Early Hudson Bay fur trading posts had tallies of about 1,500 wolverine furs purchased annually from 1752 through 1924. After that the encroachment of civilization drastically reduced wolverine numbers, until today there are just a few hundred roaming the most remote areas of the United States below the Canadian border.

Michigan, nicknamed the wolverine state, has a great abundance of a mutated species, easily located by traveling to Ann Arbor on a Saturday afternoon in fall, where wolverines can be found plastered on sweatshirts of howling University of Michigan football fans. As for the real thing, the last Michigan wolverine was seen in 1930—and shot. The extinction list reads the same for most other lower states.

Only Montana, with its vast expanses of true wilderness, still maintains a healthy wolverine population of about 200. Idaho has about 100 wolverines, and a smattering of verified sightings have come from Colorado, Washington, Wyoming, and Oregon. The vast wilderness environment of Canada and Alaska harbors a healthy wolverine population in the tens of thousands.

Often times, folks who live in the above-mentioned western states are unaware that wolverines live in their mountains. An interesting experience I've had on this subject concerned a proposed relaxing of the strict ordinance outlawing motorized vehicles within wilderness areas. A snowmobile club had petitioned the U.S. Forest Service to allow snowmobile intrusion into the Great Burn Wilderness along the Idaho/Montana border, citing the desolation of the backcountry in winter.

Conservationists complained that these remote basins were prime wolverine habitat. In response a longtime resident wrote to the local paper daring anyone to come forward with even three confirmed wolverine sightings in the Great Burn. I furnished an itemized list, dating back to 1980, of thirteen wolverines confirmed trapped or shot. I did not include the eighteen confirmed sightings because there was not irrefutable proof.

This well-meaning old-timer had spent sixty years living on the fringe of wilderness, but he had never spent a great deal of time in the farthest reaches of the backcountry. Consequently, he had never seen a wolverine because he never ventured into the animal's habitat.

Fortunately, this rule was not changed, and snowmobiles remain illegal in wilderness areas, though numerous violations occur each winter.

One of the most eye-opening wolverine studies was done by Idaho wildlife biologist Jeff Copeland. Rumors of wolverines roaming the farthest reaches of south-central Idaho's Sawtooth Mountains finally prompted a dubious state wildlife agency to spend a few bucks to investigate. What Jeff Copeland found turned a lot of heads.

From 1992 through 1995 Copeland nabbed nineteen wolverines in live traps in the high mountains of the Sawtooth, Boise, and Challis

National Forests. Surveillance of these radio-collared animals furnished much previously unknown information about the secretive life of the wolverine.

Two of the most astounding things Copeland discovered included the vastness of a wolverine's home range, and the sparse population numbers of wolverines, even in prime habitat. The average wolverine range was about 800 square miles. That's an area roughly 30 miles by 30 miles! Copeland learned that it normally took a wolverine about thirty to forty days to travel through its home rage in search of food.

Another surprising discovery was that wolverines are social animals. Because of their fierce reputation, many biologists believed that if two wolverines met they'd probably fight to the death. On the contrary Copeland found that a wolverine leaves its scent at specific spots along its travel routes, and any wolverine passing through will also leave its scent. That way these low-density (only a few per area), wide-ranging predators can readily locate each other for mating.

Most male predators will readily prey upon the young of their species, but Copeland once observed a large male wolverine entering a female's den, after which the male was seen with the young wolverines following close behind. Biologists believe this behavior allows younger wolverines to locate prime scavenging areas where experienced older animals have dug up carrion. As a result of his study, Copeland now believes that wolverines have a much more intricate and cordial social structure than previously believed—a secret society where males seek out the same females to mate every year, and older animals tolerate younger ones, thereby showing them the "who, how, when and where" of survival in a harsh environment where survival is virtually impossible—unless you're a wolverine.

Mating

The wolverine's fearsome snarl even carries over to its mating process. I once observed two wolverines mating at Northwest Trek, a natural history preserve south of Seattle. Blissful love it was not. Both animals growled fiercely and bit at each other as they rolled in a tight ball, with the male's superior size eventually pinning the female to the ground. But that sound! You'd have thought they were killing each other!

Mating season begins in mid-March, with males traveling extensively to locate females. With such a huge range to cover, this seems almost impossible, but the males and females leave their scents at specific areas, such as a dead tree along a trail, or a fork in the trail. These scent areas tell a wolverine which gender has passed through the area, and how recently.

After a brief, tumultuous mating period, two or three kits are born, sightless and covered with a wooly yellowish white fur. After eight weeks the kits are weaned and begin to follow the female; sometimes the male hangs around after the kits are born and they follow him. By October the kits have grown to almost the size of their mother, though the family unit stays together until spring, when the yearlings are chased away by a male suitor.

THE FISHER

I saw the strangest animal today," a young man mentioned as we shared a campfire at the Whistler Campground, near Jasper in Canada's Banff National Park. It was mid-September, and my focus had been on photographing bull elk during their fall mating season, but the mention of a "strange" animal sighting piqued my interest.

"What did it look like?" I asked.

"Well," the man mulled the question before responding, "It looked like a big black cat with short legs, but maybe more like a big black fox, and it had this long bushy tail. I was fishing along a creek when it loped out of the woods and spotted me. Then it took off like a shot."

"Who knows," he chuckled, "maybe I discovered a new animal. It sure didn't look like anything I've ever seen, even in nature books."

I cut short his reverie. "I think I know what it was."

The young man jerked his head back, surprised yet skeptical.

"It was a fisher."

"The young man gave me a dumbfounded look. "A what?"

That's a common response. The fisher is so rarely seen in the Rocky Mountains that few folks are even aware that it exists. But exist it does, and in numbers greater than expected.

My Extraordinary Fisher Encounter

In more than three decades of traveling some of the most remote wilderness in the Rocky Mountains, I've seen only three fishers. This doesn't mean the fisher is that rare, but it does speak to the animal's propensity to seek dense cover and to hunt either at night or at dusk, when most human activity in the backcountry has ceased.

I saw my first fisher in 1982 while camped along a remote stretch of the North Fork Clearwater River in north Idaho. The campsite was located under a dense canopy of old-growth cedar trees 6 feet in diameter. This area was always shaded and somewhat damp, with logs from past floods strewn along the stream's banks. These logs served as "rodent hotels," places where mice and rats nested and sought refuge from predators. In previous winter trips through this area I had spotted the tracks of several predators, including ermine, marten, bobcat, and coyote.

One evening I decided to go fishing, and since I was camped right along the banks of the stream, I fished until dusk. I'd caught three 14-inch cutthroats and was trying to get one more before dark. Beyond the deep pool where I'd just laid a royal coachman dry fly, I spotted a dark animal, which I initially guessed was a marten, loping along a downed tree 50 yards away on the opposite side of the stream. I stood motionless, hoping it would come my way.

The animal hopped across a series of logs and into a small opening. It was almost black, much different from the light brown martens I'd seen in Idaho, and its tail was almost twice as long. When it was 30 yards away and directly across the stream, I made a squeaking sound with my mouth. The animal stopped, and it was then that I recognized it to be a female fisher. She spotted me and disappeared in a blur.

A few years later I saw another female fisher loping along a dense stream bottom of the South Fork Flathead River near Glacier National Park. I was more than satisfied to claim two fisher sightings in my lifetime, but fate would deliver to me my own fisher to study at point blank range.

The winter of 2000 was brutal in the Rocky Mountains, with heavy snow arriving in early November and quickly building to several feet. I was living in a small cottage in northwest Montana just a few miles from the Idaho border. My living room had a massive 6- by 10-foot picture window that gave me a terrarium-like view of a high country lodgepole pine forest. In summer deer, moose, bears, and elk passed through daily. In winter it was not unusual to see coyotes, bobcats, ermine, and marten. While others cursed the deep snow, I felt blessed to sit in my living room and look out at this winter wonderland.

I was in the habit of waking before first light so I could be on hand for the stirring of the forest at dawn. One morning I padded into the living room in the dark. A full moon bathed the forest in an eerie light, allowing me to see almost 100 yards into the trees. From the dark void came an animal loping through the forest. With bated breath, I watched the dark form undulate toward me. Adrenalin shot through my veins. I thought, "A wolverine!" No, I corrected myself—too small, too long in the body. And then I recognized it to be a very large male fisher.

My binoculars were on a shelf 10 feet away, but I dared not fetch them, fearful the fisher would see the movement and be gone. He loped onto the top of a snowbank created by snow sliding off the steep metal roof and peered into the window at me. He was not more than 20 feet away. Then he was gone. My heart sank, but I reminded myself that I should be grateful for the experience.

The fisher returned and hopped back onto the snowbank and walked its length, occasionally standing on his hind legs to peer at the house and detached garage. The animal disappeared again, but a few minutes later I saw him loping into my open garage. I had a hunch that something wasn't right with the fisher. This was very unusual behavior for this shy animal, and I guessed that extreme hunger had driven him to my back door. Normally, feeding wildlife is not recommended, but I felt the fisher was in a desperate condition, possibly starving, so I hurried to the refrigerator and scanned its contents for any suitable fisher food. There was nothing but an old burger left over from yesterday's dinner. I eased the door open and threw the burger onto the snow-packed driveway in front of the garage. Moments later the fisher walked into the open, spotted the burger and stalked toward it. When he was 4 feet away, the fisher seized the meat in a blur of movement and was gone.

When the sun came up I went outside and examined the plethora of fisher tracks around the house and garage. Throughout the day I relived the delicious memories of that encounter in my mind, and wondered, "Could it happen again?"

Another storm front moved in that night and snow began to fall. The cloud cover postponed dawn the next morning, and I fidgeted for what seemed like forever until the dark faded into gloomy daybreak. The fisher had paid a visit during the night, as evidenced by the tracks in the fresh fallen snow.

Disappointed I'd missed the fisher, I started to turn away when the big male emerged from a thicket of red fir trees and loped toward the picture window. This time I was ready. I eased the back door open and threw out a fresh chicken breast. The fisher hopped onto the snow berm and stood on his hind legs, peering into the picture window at me.

As snow sifted down through the trees, the fisher and I studied each other. His dark eyes showed no sign of fear, just curiosity. I doubt he recognized me as a human. He shook the snow from his coat, which settled back into a fluffy mixture of grayish brown guard hairs along his neck and shoulders, with dark brown finer fur underneath and down his sides. Staring at the fisher from a distance of only 20 feet, I thought he was the most beautiful wild creature I'd ever seen.

He sniffed the air and followed the scent trail in a hump-backed walk along the top of the snowbank. His head jerked up when he spotted the chicken breast. In a blur he snatched it and was gone. For three more days the fisher appeared for a morning meal of venison, which I'd cut from a road-killed deer. I tried everything to capture him on film, but was frustrated by his quick, furtive movement, and the fact that he didn't stay around long enough for the light to improve.

On the fifth day I sat in the predawn gloom waiting for my new friend, but he didn't appear that morning, or the next. I never saw the fisher again, nor did I cut his tracks when I made a wide snowshoe trek around my cabin. Whatever prompted that fisher to act so brazen remains a mystery to me; most disappear at the first hint of a human's presence. He wasn't emaciated or injured. On the contrary he appeared healthy and strong.

It certainly wasn't the 6 feet of soft snow that drove him out of the high country. He easily traveled atop the white stuff. Possibly he was curious, and the availability of food kept him nearby until his instincts drove him to seek the solitude of the wilderness. Whatever the reason, my fisher encounter is one of the highlights of my outdoor life.

A Baffling Name for a Non-Fisherman

The fisher doesn't fish, so why the name? Much of the reason has been lost through history, but we do know that the first name laid on this curious animal was "Le Pekan" by French Canadian trappers in the 1700s. They were also baffled by this odd animal when they began spreading through the vast wilderness of Canada to harvest its bounty of fur. Other names laid on this animal were black cat, tree fox, black fox, pekan weasel, fisher cat, and fisher-marten.

This plethora of names grew from the confusion among Hudson Bay traders because a female fisher closely approximated a marten in size and color. Fisher-marten became the most popular name that trappers and fur traders used as a means of differentiating the two species.

The "fisher" moniker became more popular among trappers because, unlike the marten, which prefers the high dense forest, the fisher is most often found near streams or swamps. Some early naturalists erred in guessing that the fisher traveled along waterways to catch fish. On the contrary the fisher lurks in these areas because they are prime hunting grounds for rodents.

The Fisher Is an Exceptional Hunter

A fisher's lightning-quick reflexes and aggressive nature make it the scourge of the prey base wherever it roams. Few prey animals can escape a determined effort by a fisher. The one critter that gives a fisher a good run is the snowshoe hare. The fisher's oversize paws also carry it over the deep snow, so a footrace between fisher and hare is close. And when the hare dives into a dense thicket that frustrates a bobcat or lynx, the narrow-bodied fisher dives right in after it.

Sometimes the hunt is long and protracted. A homesteader who was traveling along the shore of Great Slave Lake, Northwest Territories, recounted how he saw a large fisher in pursuit of a snowshoe hare. The speedy hare stayed well ahead of the predator. But the hare, insecure beyond its recognized home territory, began running in a wide circle back to its willow thicket, a circle that became smaller every time it made the rounds. The fisher kept pace with the hare by staying on a course within that circle, which allowed it to cover less ground to keep up. Finally, the fisher cut across the ever-narrowing circle and, with an astonishing burst of speed, pounced on the tired hare.

The snowshoe hare comprises about 10 percent of a fisher's diet, while mice and red squirrels account for the bulk of it, along with an occasional duck or grouse. Mice and pack rats are creatures of the night, so the fisher becomes virtually nocturnal when hunting them. The red squirrel, on the other hand, is most active during the early and late hours of the day, and the fisher who hunts it is more prone to be seen in daylight hours. A red squirrel is fast and reckless as it soars through the trees, but much to its surprise, and demise, the squirrel discovers the fisher is also a good climber and kills about every third squirrel it chases.

The Fisher and the Porcupine

One of the most amazing things about this most extraordinary animal is its penchant for killing and eating the porcupine with no ill effects. Other predators, such as the mountain lion, bobcat, lynx, and wolverine, suffer miserably when they make the mistake of pouncing on a "porky," whose needle-sharp, barbed quills stay embedded in the hide and muscle and cause great pain, swelling, and usually a slow, torturous death. One wilderness traveler tells of finding a large male mountain lion near death lying alongside a trail. The lion's paws, face and neck were full of porcupine quills and the swelling was severe.

The fisher, on the other hand, seldom has a problem with porcupine quills because it slips a paw under the animal's belly and flips it onto its back, exposing its vulnerable underbelly. And when a fisher does get stuck, the quills have no adverse effect. Necropsies on fishers have found no swelling around the hide or muscle where quills had entered; when the fisher's intestines were opened up, packs of quills were found in tight bundles making their way through the mucous membrane without puncturing it.

The fisher is so fond of porcupine flesh that, when it is abundant, the fisher preys almost exclusively on this slow-moving animal. A naturalist studying fishers in Canada discovered where a female fisher had killed three porcupines in a creek bottom in a single morning. The predator ate only a small portion of neck meat from each porcupine.

Fishers Occasionally Kill Large Animals

It seems ludicrous that an eighteen-pound fisher could kill a deer or caribou weighing more than one hundred pounds. Yet several stories of fishers preying on these animals have come from wilderness travelers. This story comes from the famous naturalist, Ernest Thompson Thomas Seton, in his book *Lives of Game Animals*. Hunter Louis Ketcham was tracking a big buck in northern Canada on a snowy morning. Along a narrow rock ledge, Ketcham found where the buck had fallen, and there was blood on the snow. The deer had then regained its feet and stumbled along a few steps before falling again, where there was more blood on the snow. This happened several more times and then, from the disturbance in the snow, Ketcham guessed that the buck had finally dislodged a big male fisher and gored it with its antlers. Ketcham found the fisher dragging its hind legs, undoubtedly injured in the attack.

Predators Are Few

Many larger predators have the potential to prey on a fisher—if they could catch it. At the first hint of danger, a fisher scurries up a tree, leaving only the mountain lion and bobcat as serious threats. But the fisher is so adept at soaring between trees that these wild cats are usually left behind. When caught on the ground, a fisher is able to squeeze into a hole or rocky crevice barely 5 inches wide, and God help the wolverine or bobcat that sticks its nose into that hole—a fisher is a tenacious fighter when cornered and would cause serious injury to the faces of those predators.

Man is the only serious predator of the fisher. In the past, fisher hides have fetched high prices. And since the fisher is not trap-shy, it readily comes in to a baited trap set by men who penetrate the fringes of the wilderness.

Incidental trapping and the encroachment of civilization have led to the decline, and even extermination, of fisher populations in many areas of the Rockies. A few years back, the Montana Department of Fish, Wildlife and Parks targeted the remote Bull River drainage west of the Cabinet Mountains Wilderness Area in northwestern Montana as prime habitat for fisher and initiated an ambitious reintroduction program. Unfortunately, the Bull River Road ran along this stream, and many of these fishers were caught in leghold traps set for bobcats.

Species Description

Anyone who has seen a fisher is truly blessed, because this predator is nocturnal, or nearly so, depending on the prey it seeks. The fisher is most active at the times when humans are usually in camp or asleep. Those fortunate observers of the fisher still have trouble explaining exactly what they saw, as was the case with my young friend in Banff National Park. Expeditioners Lewis and Clark had the same problem, calling the fisher "black fox" or "tree fox," because of its tendency to take to the trees when startled or hunting, and also because of its resemblance to the silver fox in the East (a rare black mutation of the red fox).

A fisher has a smooth, loping gait, much like a cat. Hence, people who see a fisher often mistake it for a large black cat. So fast are its movements that most folks who see a fisher never get the chance to study it closely before it disappears into the forest, which is exactly what this animal does immediately upon encountering a human.

An adult male fisher has short legs and a long, muscular body, and a long bushy tail. Its fur is dark brown in color, but males have whitish guard hairs along the neck and shoulders which give them a grizzled look. A fisher's face is foxlike—narrow with a pointed snout and smallish round ears. Males weigh about twelve to eighteen pounds, but look much larger because of their elongated body and long tail. Females are a third the size of males, and their fur is almost black in color, with no whitish guard hairs.

Habitat

Other than the mysterious appearance of the big male fisher at the back door of my cabin, I've never heard of a fisher hanging around civilization. This shy, retreating animal is usually found in the most remote habitat far back from roads and towns in the lower country. During my winter travels in search of fisher sign, I have never cut a fisher track close to civilization. Instead, I usually find fisher tracks at the heads of remote drainages where humans rarely travel.

Normally, a fisher lives in dense, high-country creek bottoms, where hares and squirrels are abundant. It hunts logjams and overturned tree roots for mice and keeps an eye above for red squirrels. Most of the fisher tracks I find are in these gloomy creek bottoms. It also visits rock outcrops in its home range to hunt for pack rats and mice. The fisher's favorite food, the porcupine, likes to eat the sappy bark from new trees growing in areas that have been burned, and a fisher will readily roam through these thickets of young trees.

Range and Population

The fisher is mostly a high-country dweller of the northern Rockies. Its range extends to Great Slave Lake in northern Canada, and southward to Yellowstone National Park and the northwest tip of Wyoming. I've traveled much of the high country in Wyoming, Colorado, Utah, and New Mexico and have found that, despite an abundance of red squirrels, the fisher is absent from these states. Wildlife biologists are at a loss to explain why.

A fisher's home range is normally about 2 square miles, which the animal covers in a tireless, impatient lope. Within that area live thousands of red squirrels, mice, rats, and snowshoe hares to eat. However, biologists following two radio-collared fishers noted that the animals occasionally wandered away from their home range to another mountain 2 miles away. This may have been due to poor hunting in their home, or because they were being chased by another invading fisher or a larger predator.

The fisher, like the wolverine, is not abundant anywhere, but from my observations while snowshoeing through the backcountry in winter, there is a light scattering of fishers in the high country throughout the Rocky Mountains in Montana and Idaho. A small population of fishers also live in the northern Cascade Mountains in Washington and Oregon. The vast wilderness of Canada holds a stable population, with fishers in evidence up to the southern limits of Great Slave Lake in Northwest Territories.

In my opinion, the fisher, and its near relative, the wolverine, are true harbingers of wilderness because they seek the most remote expanses of the Rockies. To view a fisher loping along a log is a true wilderness experience to be treasured for a lifetime. Then again, there are some of us who find them at the back door!

Mating

Fishers mate in early March, and following conception, the female keeps the inch-long babies in a small pouch inside her womb until the nasty spring weather in the Rockies eases. A typical litter is two to five kits, born sightless and with a covering of downy brown fur. As soon as the kits can travel, they accompany their mother on the hunt and learn valuable skills, such as how to turn a porcupine on its back. Sometime during the fall months, with the kits half-grown and capable of catching mice and squirrels on their own, the family unit dissolves as the young wander off to claim their own hunting territory.

THE MARTEN

My friend Bud Molle's first marten experience was unusual, to say the least. Bud was on an elk-hunting trip with friends in the wilderness of central Idaho, and one of the men had killed a bull elk the first day. The carcass was cut into quarters and hung from a stout pole lashed between two spruce trees. The temperature dipped well below freezing that first night, and the meat was partially frozen by morning. Before they embarked on their hunt, the outfitter fitted muslin sheets loosely over the quarters to shield them from marauding jays and the sun, which might warm the meat and cause it to spoil.

With the meat in such fine shape, it was largely ignored by the men in the camp—except for Bud Molle. "I'd look at this one elk quarter, a rear ham. It seemed to be moving, swaying, twisting—even though there wasn't any breeze. The other quarters sure weren't moving. They were frozen solid. Another thing was the size of the quarter. It seemed to be shrinking, and the muslin was hanging looser and looser every time I looked at it.

"One day after the morning hunt, I noticed the elk quarter jerking and twisting. I walked over and raised the cloth. There was a 2-inch hole right in the middle of it. When I leaned forward to look into it, this marten pokes its head out, sees me, and lets out a blood-curdling scream. And then I let out my own blood-curdling scream."

"We finally got rid of the marten, and when we cut into that rear ham, we found that the marten had chewed a large hole out of the center of it and it looked to me like it was living in there. There was probably twenty pounds of meat missing."

A Family Pet

A most unusual marten story came to me from Denver residents Larry and Wendy Wisenman, who purchased a vacation cabin in 2002 near Estes Park, which borders Rocky Mountain National Park 40 miles north of Denver. The place hadn't been lived in for almost a year and was infested with pack rats and squirrels. Larry tried to trap them, without much success. Wendy, in the meantime, was terrified to sleep there. "As soon as the lights went out," she laments, "the pack rats would start scampering across the floor, across the kitchen table, across the bed. I told Larry I just couldn't sleep there anymore."

The cabin needed some repair, so Larry started driving up there on weekends to work on the place. "At first, the rats and squirrels drove me nuts, but then it seemed like their activity dropped off. I thought maybe I was just getting used to it, but I started noticing a lot less droppings around the place.

"One evening I heard a scraping noise in the ceiling, but it sounded kind of different. Then a head pokes through a hole that the squirrels had chewed through a corner of the ceiling. This pointy-faced critter looks around, and then hops onto the top of the cupboard and in one leap is across the room. When it saw me it screeched and went back up through the hole in the ceiling so fast I couldn't believe it."

Larry flipped through some natural history books and identified the visitor as a marten. He saw the marten the next evening loping along the porch, sniffing dark corners where Larry had seen pack rats emerge. The more Larry read about the marten as a supreme hunter of rodents and squirrels, the more he became convinced that the marten was eliminating the pests. Eventually, he was able to convince Wendy to return to the cabin, and she was ecstatic to spend the night there without a pack rat hopping across the bed. Of course, it took her a while to get used to "Red," as they named the marten, making occasional sweeps through the cabin.

Red has been a frequent visitor to the Wisenman's cabin for the past three years, and they are thrilled with the notion that this deep woods predator has taken up residence near their home. "Sometimes," Wendy mentions, "Red visits us when we're barbecuing, usually with friends. Red climbs through the trees, staring down at us, and sniffing at the barbecue smells. We thought about feeding him, but we'd read that it wasn't a good idea to start feeding animals, especially since there's black bears in the area."

A Valuable Fur

From the earliest days of the Hudson Bay Company, the marten was pursued for its silky fur. In the 1700s French-Canadian and native trappers used crude deadfalls before steel traps were used. A deadfall was made using a heavy stone or log, with a baited stick holding up the heavy weight. When the marten tugged on the bait, it was crushed.

Steel traps came into use in the 1800s and accelerated the marten harvest. Literally tens of millions of marten pelts were shipped to European markets through the years by the Hudson Bay Company. Fur garments made with marten fur were often labeled as "sable," the term commonly used in the fur industry for the more lustrous Russian marten. While the demand for other furs has risen and fallen with the fickleness of the fashion world, sable fur has always been in demand.

In the early 1900s marten furs sold for $6.00 to $12.00 dollars, a whopping price back then. The marten was pursued relentlessly by trappers, and many areas were greatly reduced due to overtrapping because the marten is not trap-shy and will readily come to any baited trap.

Pioneer naturalist Ernest Thompson Seton, a hunter and trapper himself, lamented the full-scale slaughter of martens in the 1920s for their fur and wrote, "Man, of course, is the chief enemy of the marten. In all my records of observations, I do not know of one case in which a man came in contact with a marten without trying to kill it. Kill, kill, kill, for the lust of slaughter, even when no profit could be reaped in the way of fur or protection of livestock. The annual slaughter is somewhere around 100,000 martens each year, and this counts only the prime skins taken in season."

The good news is that fur garments, including sable, are not as popular as they once were. Though fur garments have come back into style the past few years, the expensive furs, such as sable, will probably never garner the tremendous demand of the 1920s, when every high-class lady had to have a sable garment. The result is that the marten's numbers have returned to normal throughout much of its historic range.

The Marten's Prey Base

The red squirrel is always in danger if a marten lives in the same woods. The marten's tree-climbing ability is as good as the squirrel's, and its longer body allows it to gain quickly on any fleeing squirrel. The fox and gray squirrel are twice as large as the red squirrel, but they are also slower and fall easy prey to a marten. Undoubtedly, the absence of these larger squirrels in the wilderness is a result of their slowness in escaping predators.

In the red squirrel's home range, it sets up a pinecone cache where it feels safe, and visits the cache several times daily to dig up and eat cones.

Eventually, a huge pile of discarded cone hulls builds up, and the squirrel uses this as an observation point, sitting atop it while munching on cone seeds. Unfortunately, these cone dumps are also the focal point for the hunting marten. It ceases its helter-skelter movement when it gets close to a cone dump and eases forward to inspect the area for a squirrel.

The chase is chaotic, with the screeching squirrel running for its life. The marten keeps after the squirrel until it is caught. The only hope for the squirrel is to dive into a hole small enough to keep a larger marten out, but a smaller female or half-grown marten will follow the squirrel right into the hole and kill it.

It is my opinion that the red squirrel is the favorite prey of the tree-loving marten, but it comprises only about half of its diet. The snowshoe hare is another prey favorite. The hare is faster, but the marten stays after it, often for an hour or more, until the hare tires. Any hole or dense tangle the desperate hare dives into will be manageable for the slimmer marten. Mice, rats, and voles make up the rest of the marten's diet. It hunts these animals in log jumbles or rock piles.

The marten is also a great bird hunter, taking grouse and smaller birds, which it hunts in trees and on the ground. When berries ripen, a marten will crawl into the bushes and lie motionless until a bird appears and begins pecking at the fruit. When the bird gets within 6 feet, the marten attacks in a blur of movement and snatches the birds from the bush. I've seen martens hunting birds in huckleberry bushes with great success. They lie in the dense tangle under the bush, and the bird, hopping along the top of the bush where the fruit grows, become easy prey.

Every predator has a quirk of nature that it alone possesses to aid it in its hunt for food. With the lynx and bobcat, it's ear tufts that act as radar; with the wolverine it's an extraordinary sense of smell. When prey is in short supply, or when a marten is slowed by injury, it seeks out fresh dirt mounds in a meadow where moles are tunneling. The dense fur on the bottom of the marten's paws enables it to detect the slightest vibration, which leads it to the underground location of a burrowing mole. There, the marten sits motionless, watching for the slightest disturbance. When it spots fresh dirt pushing up, it dives in and digs furiously until it unearths the hapless mole.

Marten as Prey

Averaging only about three pounds, a marten must keep one eye searching for animals to kill and eat, and the other searching for predators that want to kill and eat it. That's probably why the marten is always in motion, knowing that the longer it stays in one place, the greater the chances of something bigger, faster, stronger pouncing on it. The marten's affinity for trees not only furnishes prime hunting, but also keeps it above the host of predators that lurk below.

There is one predator that takes to the trees as readily as the marten. The fisher is just a wee bit faster, bigger, and stronger than a marten, and will kill a marten if given the chance. However, a marten is no pushover, and a fisher is likely to expend so much time and energy chasing a marten all over the forest that it seeks the marten as prey only when a golden opportunity arises.

A marten must leave the safety of the trees when it moves from one stand to another, or when it is hunting snowshoe hares in thickets, or mice in log jumbles. On the ground it occasionally falls prey to bobcats, lynx, and fishers. Larger predators such as the mountain lion, wolf, wolverine, and bear are not quick enough to catch a darting marten. Young marten also fall to birds of prey, such as large hawks and eagles.

A marten is particularly vulnerable when it hunts the snowshoe hare because it must stay on the trail of the hare for an extended period, during which time it is less able to watch out for predators. When a lynx hunting the same thicket becomes aware of a marten chasing a hare, it quickly moves into position and waits in ambush. If the hare presents an opportunity, so much the better, but if it's the marten that bounds by within striking range, the lynx is only too happy to dine on sable.

A surprisingly common cause of marten mortality is the pitch that oozes from spruce, pine, and fir trees in the deep forest. This sappy liquid smears over the marten's fur as it roams through the trees, and eventually hardens. When winter arrives, with its deep snow and bitter cold, the marten's pitch-balled fur cannot insulate it from the weather and it succumbs to the elements.

Species Description

The marten moves through the forest so swiftly that most folks aren't sure exactly what animal they saw. This confusion stems from the fact that most marten are seen in trees, immediately leading a hiker to think she or he has seen a very large red squirrel.

A mature red squirrel weighs about a half pound, while a marten weighs about four pounds. Marten fur in the lower states is generally silky in texture and brown in color. The farther north you go, the marten's fur becomes darker and its size increases. Alaska marten weigh up to six pounds, and their fur is dark brown.

A marten's face looks very similar to the face of a red fox, with a pointed nose and beady black eyes and large grayish ears. The distinguishing mark of a marten is the bright orange throat patch, which is so light on some marten that it is almost tan.

A mature male marten's body is weasel-like. It is about 2 feet long and slim, with short legs for sudden bursts of speed, and a dark brown, bushy tail half as long as its body. Females are a bit smaller. Its paws are oversize and act as snowshoes to keep the marten on top of the snow. At the end of each paw are tiny white claws that dig into a tree trunk or the flimsiest limb and allow the marten to safely travel with speed and ease through the trees.

A marten track resembles a fox track (which resembles a small dog's track), but is distinctive in the snow because it shows up as a lope with staggered paws. The left paw is always about 2 inches ahead of the right paw, with the leaps about every 4 feet. This is a quick way to tell the difference between a marten track and those of a mink or ermine, the tracks of which show the paws as even rather than staggered.

Habitat

Because marten are plentiful in the northern Rockies and quite curious by nature, most folks who have spent much time in the backcountry can relate a tale of a sleeping bag jerking to and fro and a screeching marten emerging, or a marten hopping out of the food pantry in a tent camp, or a nosy marten perching on a limb above a campsite and watching with a mixture of curiosity and envy as the people below eat their dinner.

That's not to say the marten is a found everywhere in the Rockies, for its habitat is very specific. Marten do not live along streams, like the fisher, or seek the dense thickets like a lynx, or scour avalanche chutes for carrion like their cousin the wolverine. Instead, the marten is found in deep forest, usually Douglas fir or spruce.

A marten spends half its life in the trees, usually chasing red squirrels or lying in ambush for an unwary bird. So effortless is the marten's progress as it navigates from tree to tree that the animal appears to be flying. Almost never still, the marten lopes along a limb 50 feet above the ground and launches itself through the air to another limb in a tree 30 feet away. From there it scurries up the tree, then down the tree, and then off to the next in its inexhaustible lope.

Marten prefer the seclusion of wilderness. In fact early naturalists claimed the marten was such a recluse that it would not mate or give birth if its wilderness habitat was disturbed. One naturalist gravely noted, "When the axe is laid to the deep forest by a settler, every marten in the area immediately leaves."

However, I've found that marten sometimes travel through fringe areas. In western Montana's Big Hole River Valley, I once followed the tracks of a marten that left a lodgepole pine forest and traveled through a series of clearcuts. Though this maneuver exposed the marten to predators, it became obvious the animal took the risk because the clearcuts included many piles of unburned logging debris, where pack rats and mice were in abundance.

Occasionally I've found marten near civilization. I once spotted a marten hunting along a finger of spruce trees a half mile above the ski resort town of Steamboat Springs, Colorado. The marten had a great view of this bustling town, but it ignored the sounds and sights, more intent on finding a red squirrel for dinner.

If prey is plentiful or if a winter-killed large animal offers the chance for an easy meal, marten may converge on an area. I've been surprised, upon entering a secluded forest, to find the snow crisscrossed with fresh marten tracks. More often than not I'm able to follow them to a dead elk or moose the marten are feeding on. On a few occasions I've found where a mountain lion had killed a deer, and one or more marten had moved in and helped themselves to the lion's kill. The lion is much too slow to catch a speedy marten, so the lion usually ignores a marten that pilfers, at most, a half pound of meat.

Range and Population

The marten is found mainly in the northern Rockies, ranging all the way to the barren slopes of Alaska and south into southern Idaho and south-western Wyoming until the coniferous forests give way to scrub oak and juniper. Where the coniferous forests of spruce and pine reappear farther south in Colorado and northern New Mexico, so does the marten.

Marten populations don't experience the drastic boom-and-bust cycle of the snowshoe hare, but their numbers do fluctuate depending upon the availability of prey; so when the hare is in short supply, marten numbers dip somewhat, and when hares are plentiful, so are marten. This tendency showed up during a recent furbearer snow survey taken by the Montana Department of Fish, Wildlife & Parks in the Great Bear Wilderness Area. A snow survey is one of the most precise methods of counting reclusive furbearers because of their telltale tracks left in the snow.

During the Montana snow survey, researchers skied about 45 miles around Shafer Meadows in the Middle Fork of the Flathead River. They counted a whopping 1,196 sets of snowshoe hare tracks and 162 different marten tracks, 320 sets of red squirrel tracks, fifty-six sets of ermine tracks, eleven mountain coyote tracks, no mountain lion tracks (because the lions had migrated to lower country to escape the deep snow), no wolverine, and fifteen sets of lynx tracks.

While these numbers are not scientifically significant, they are a good indication of how the furbearers in the wilderness are faring. "Marten were everywhere," one researcher noted. "And one interesting thing about the marten in the Great Bear Wilderness was that they did a lot of their hunting on the ground, and under the snow for red-backed voles."

This survey showed an average of three martens per mile traveled, which is about three times greater than the average I've found during my personal marten treks. No doubt the increased marten and lynx numbers were the result of a high snowshoe-hare population.

It is one of the joys of my life to traverse the high-country forests on snowshoes in the dead of winter after a fresh snow to search for marten tracks. On a normal trek that covers about 8 miles, I'll spot an average of about eight sets of marten tracks. That's one marten per mile, which is the normal range for this species, with larger males often expanding their range to 2 square miles.

Mating

Like most members of the weasel family, marten don't socialize, and the only time they seek out their kind is during mating season. The males, who normally avoid each other, often fight viciously for the right to mate a receptive female. Mating usually occurs in late February or early March, when the backcountry is still bitter cold and buried under deep snow. Marten young would quicky die in these conditions, so Nature has provided by allowing the mating process to take place when warm spring days melt the snow and leave a hard crust on top, allowing extensive travel for male martens seeking females.

Nature further ensures for the welfare of the marten young by postponing the implant of the embryos into the female's uterus for about two months, while the male's sperm has been incubating. When two to six marten kits are born, most of the snow has melted, and the temperature is well above freezing.

Baby marten are born with their eyes closed and their bodies covered with a soft, whitish down, which quickly begins to turn light brown. A few weeks after their eyes are open, the young marten begin trailing after their mother during her hunts and thereby learn where and how to locate various prey species. In fall the family unit dissolves when the half-grown marten are capable of killing mice and squirrels on their own.

THE ERMINE

The plump brown deer mouse scampered across the snow, its tiny legs churning madly. Twenty feet behind it a sleek white ermine bounded, gaining rapidly on the mouse. An instant before the ermine pounced on it, the mouse disappeared below the snow. The ermine hopped back and forth, frantically searching for the mouse, then dove into the snow in pursuit.

From my perch under a large cedar tree 40 feet away, it appeared the hunt was over. Suddenly the mouse popped up and scurried straight toward me. The ermine erupted in a shower of snow next to a fir sapling. It shook the snow off its muzzle, spotted the mouse and loped after it, but the rodent once again dove below the surface just ahead of the ermine.

The mouse broke the surface 4 feet to my left and ran for about 5 feet before it tunneled beneath the snow again. A second later the ermine emerged and followed the mouse's trail into the hole. Seconds went by. Then the mouse flew into the air with the ermine just 2 feet behind it. Both animals dove into the snow again, and I heard a muffled, "Squeak!"

I waited for a minute without seeing any action. As I was turning away, the ermine's head popped up. It looked around, grabbed the mouse and bounded across the snow to a large cedar log and disappeared.

Is It a Weasel or an Ermine?

The ermine is one of those animals that keeps us in awe of the wisdom of Mother Nature. To begin with, it's not only an ermine, but it's also a weasel. For seven months of the year, when the Rockies are free of snow, this diminutive animal is simply a weasel—brown in color, with a white throat patch. But when late fall arrives, a startling metamorphosis occurs. In just a few days, the drab brown weasel changes into a dazzling white ermine. Of course, it's the same animal. The name, "ermine," is just the term given to the white color phase of the weasel.

We owe much to the early naturalists of the early 1900s who paved the way for modern natural science, but some of their observations and conclusions were flawed. Naturalist George Shiras wrote of the ermine, "We were camped in Newfoundland in November 1907. We began feeding six brown weasels that had begun to hang around camp. Then came a snow. The day after the storm ended, there were six ermines bounding around camp. In my opinion, they did not, and could not have changed overnight. Instead, it was other white weasels that had already changed, who had been hiding till the snow came, and the brown ones then went into hiding until their change to white had been completed." Hmm!

Scientists now know this sudden change in appearance is the result of a rapid molt, and has nothing to do with the season or the presence of snow. I've seen a half dozen ermines loping along the bare ground in November, looking very conspicuous in their winter white coats against the brown terrain. It may look out of place, but the ermine's new coat doesn't appear to hamper its hunting ability.

However, not all weasels turn white. On the west slopes of the Cascade Mountains in British Columbia, the Pacific influence creates a temperate rainforest habitat, where snow is infrequent, and the weasels here do not turn white in winter. And in the southern Rockies, where snow is almost unheard of, the weasel remains brown year-round.

One late November afternoon I was driving up an old logging road in the Fish Creek drainage near the Great Burn Wilderness in western Montana. I saw a rabbit crossing the road about 30 yards ahead. But something was very wrong. The rabbit was on its back. I threw up my binoculars and grunted in surprise. The rabbit was dead and was being pulled across the road by an ermine—a very white one.

I grabbed my camera and followed the ermine as it frantically tugged and dragged that rabbit over rugged terrain. Finally, it had enough of my interference. With its tail puffed out to show agitation, it stood erect and hissed menacingly at me. I backed off and it quickly pulled the rabbit into a crevasse in the rocks.

Seldom Seen by Man

The ermine is most visible when deep snow covers the backcountry. Even with its white coat, an ermine is easily seen loping across the snow. I've seen dozens of ermines in my winter travels, but during this time of year most humans are huddled in their cozy homes far from the wilderness and therefore seldom see the creature at that time.

When summer arrives and hikers and campers filter into the wilderness, the ermine is no more, having been transformed into the brown weasel, which spends most of its time hunting in the low brush that covers the land. In more than three decades of tramping through the Rockies, I've seen only four weasels in summer. Most weasels at this time appear along the fringes of the backcountry near dwellings. In some ways that's good, because a weasel rids the outbuildings of vermin. But in years past the cry, "Weasel!" was a call to arms.

Early Settlers Loathed the Ermine

Early-day settlers generally loathed the weasel and considered it a cunning, bloodthirsty killer to be shot on sight. And for good reason. A century ago, these hardy folks lived virtually on the edge of starvation and relied on wild meat, along with domestic fowl and stock, to survive. Chickens were an important food source, providing eggs and white meat, which was much desired as an alternative to the drudgery of red meat.

A weasel in the chicken coop was something to be feared. A ¾-inch crack between boards was enough to allow a weasel to squeeze through and gain entrance to the coop at night after the chickens had roosted. The aftermath was often devastating. Naturalist John Bachman wrote, "In one night 40 well-grown fowls were killed by a single ermine. Satiated with the blood of probably a single fowl, the rest were destroyed in obedience to a law of nature, and instinctive propensity to kill." Bachman also noted that in a single night and the early part of the following evening, a weasel killed nearly fifty chickens, several of which were adults, and many half-grown.

This orgy of killing in the chicken coop is not limited to the ermine. A few years back, a neighbor asked me to help find out what had been killing his chickens, suspecting it was a weasel. In three nights, thirteen chickens had been killed. When I investigated, I found the tracks of a smallish bobcat, which I snared and released 5 miles away.

Ermine Are Supreme Mousers

Ermine hunt birds, squirrels, and snowshoe hares with some success. However, the hare can usually outrun an ermine. Most hares are killed by ermines when they are cornered in a thicket or den. An ermine is also adept at climbing, but for some reason rarely takes to the trees after the red squirrel. Most squirrels are killed on the ground, and the ermine is a common visitor to the cone dumps where squirrels congregate.

The bulk of the weasel's diet is mice. The tiny holes that mice enter to avoid the fisher, the bobcat, and the marten are easily entered by the slim ermine. Its favorite hunting areas are log jumbles and rock piles.

I recently read an article stating that ermine and marten hunt rodents under the snow. This gives the impression that these predators tunnel blindly beneath the snow and grope along searching for mice. This is inaccurate: They would starve to death using this tactic. Instead, an ermine mooches around a log pile, or the well of a tree or sapling that rodents routinely use as a ladder to reach the surface of the snow.

When the ermine catches the scent of a mouse, it follows the smell down through the snow to the tiny trails these rodents create along the top of the ground. (Immediately after the snow melts in spring, you can see these rodent runs until grass and foliage cover them.) When the mouse realizes it is being pursued, it then may scurry to the surface of the snow to escape the ermine, and a chase much like the one I witnessed ensues.

Ermine Predators Are Many

The ermine's fate is often sealed by its weight. It may be the toughest, fiercest fighter, pound for pound, of any predator in the Rockies, but it still weighs only a half-pound, and the amount of damage it can inflict on another predator is minimal. The most severe injury a wolf or lion will receive when it pounces on an ermine is a few tooth marks on the muzzle or paw before powerful jaws crush the life out of the brave, but doomed, ermine.

A lynx, bobcat, or big male fisher probably don't have much to fear from an ermine, either, but as the predators become smaller, they must make a more calculated decision before taking on an ermine. A female fisher or marten might decide it is not worth the potential risk if the ermine is a larger long-tailed weasel.

One winter in western Montana I observed a smallish marten backing away from a confrontation with a large ermine. It was in late November during hunting season, and I'd discovered a bend along a gravel forest road where several elk and deer carcasses had been thrown over the road bank after hunters had removed most of the meat from the bones. There was still a lot of meat left for scavengers and predators.

I dragged the carcasses into the dense forest to a small opening where I could sit back and observe. The next day there were bobcat and coyotes tracks around the carcasses. The next morning I arrived at first light and scared a marten away from the carcass. Within minutes the marten, a large male, returned and began gnawing on the semi-frozen meat clinging to a thigh bone.

An ermine about 12 inches long hopped into view, saw the marten, and circled around the carcass before edging forward. The marten spotted the ermine and bounded after it, but quit after chasing the ermine about 20 feet. No doubt this marten acted instinctively, rather than as a predator, because it had plenty of food.

Eventually, the big marten filled his belly and loped off. Within minutes, the ermine reappeared and attacked a rib cage. Then a smallish female marten appeared in a tree above the carcasses and studied the area for a few minutes before scurrying down the tree. The marten and ermine eyed each other warily for a minute, then the female marten loped around to the other side of the carcasses and began gnawing on a chunk of meat hanging from the neck of a deer. The ermine went back to chewing on the rib cage.

That female marten probably could have killed the ermine, but the fight would not have ended quickly, as it would have with the big male marten, and the ermine could have inflicted enough damage to the female to have crippled, or at least slowed her on future hunts. In my opinion, the female decided it wasn't worth the risk.

Of course, large predators are fully capable of killing an ermine with a single bite. But first they must catch it, and therein lies the great equalizer in the food chain among predators. The smaller the predator the faster it moves, and the more difficult it is to catch. I doubt even a male fisher has much success catching the speedy, darting ermine, though I've found evidence where a female fisher killed and ate an ermine. The marten, too, is small enough and fast enough to catch and kill an ermine.

Birds of prey routinely hunt ermines. A researcher studying snowy owls in Alaska noted that he often found ermine skulls in the owl's pellet stations under its roost tree. Hawks and eagles also prey upon smaller ermines. One interesting story about an ermine meeting its doom happened in Canada. As recorded by naturalist Tom McIlwraith, a young man examined a dead bald eagle and found an unusual ball hanging from the underside of its neck. Upon closer inspection, he identified it as the skull of an ermine, its teeth embedded in the eagle's neck skin. McIlwraith guessed that the eagle had pounced on the ermine and the animal had fought to its last breath, finally clamping onto the eagle's neck in a final act of defiance before expiring.

Another story from Canada, this one quite preposterous, is that an Indian shot a moose and found a dead weasel clinging to its throat. My guess is that the ermine, starving and desperate, happened upon the moose bedded in deep snow and bit into it. The moose probably rolled on the ground, or rubbed its neck against a tree and killed the ermine, which stayed clamped onto the moose's throat in a death grip.

Ermine Versus Man

An ermine's initial response to a confrontation with man is to flee, but when faced with no recourse but to fight, its utter defiance in the face of certain death also pertains to man. A humorous (though not for the ermine) story is from Ernest Thompson Seton's *Journal of the Far North*. His party of men were canoeing up the Athabaska River and had camped for the night. As the men sat around the campfire, Seton heard the soft patter of paws on leaves behind the tent. He wrote:

> I urged the men to remain motionless and silent. Out of the gloom bounded a snow-white ermine. A man named Preble was lying on his back with his hands clasped behind his head, and the ermine fearlessly jumped onto Preble's broad chest and stood peering about.

> In a flash, Preble brought his left hand down and seized the ermine, before also wrapping his right hand around the squirming animal. Preble, called excitedly, "I've got him!" Then he howled in pain and added, "But he's got me, too! Suffering Moses! The little cuss is grinding his teeth into me."

The ermine had sunk its teeth into Preble's right thumb and would not let go. Preble, wincing in pain, had no choice but to squeeze with all his might until the ermine expired. But each time Preble thought the ermine was dead, it would revive and bite down even harder on his thumb. It was a long, drawn-out affair before the ermine's body was finally crushed by Preble, who had by then become quite desperate to get the little cuss's teeth out of his thumb.

Head for the Hills to Find an Ermine!

The ermine is the most populous and easily identifiable wilderness predator. At anywhere from six to ten per mile, you can't go far without happening upon the tiny paw prints of an ermine bounding across the snow. And maybe if you're lucky, you'll even see a dazzling white ermine loping through its snowy world. Finding ermine tracks is the easiest way to become privy to the fascinating world of the wilderness predator in the Rockies.

Species Description

Most ermine are about 10 inches long, with a 4-inch, black-tipped tail. However, I've occasionally seen ermine twice that size. The smaller ermine are short-tailed weasels, while the larger are long-tailed weasels. These are the most common variety found in the Rockies.

Both of these species carry a strong musk gland at the base of the tail. When excited or frightened, they squirt a musk as putrid as that of a skunk. This musk stains the fur yellow at the base of the tail. Some ermine also have a yellowish stain about their head, which is the result of tucking their head under the base of the tail when they curl up to sleep.

An ermine track is easy to identify. They lope much like a marten, but the paws are not staggered, being instead even, with about a 2-foot spacing between lopes. Ermine tracks are sometimes confused with red squirrel tracks because they have a similar gait. However, a red squirrel's paws show the toes spread out like any rodent, while an ermine's paws resembles those of a tiny canine.

Habitat

Ermine prefer log jumbles, not only because of the abundance of small rodents, but also because the ermine can escape into the tightly packed logs when a larger predator gives chase. Every log or blown-down tree is inspected by the ermine as it passes through its hunting area. Unlike other predators who hunt by sight, the ermine hunts by both sight and scent, and is tiny enough to follow a mouse back into its nest and kill it.

I've followed hundreds of ermine tracks in winter, and the one thing that struck me was the fact that whenever an ermine ventured into the open, it was taking great leaps, no doubt because of the plethora of predators, both furred and feathered, that prey upon this tiny predator when it exposes itself.

Range and Population

Ermine are much more numerous than marten. My snow surveys show about six ermine tracks per mile traveled. Researchers estimated that the average is five to ten ermine per square mile. My guess for the high ermine numbers, as compared to marten at one per mile, is due to the fact that they are small and need only a single mouse every other day to survive.

Weasels are common throughout the Rockies, ranging to the farthest reaches of these mountains where they end in treeless tundra, and down through the southern Rockies. This is an animal that is found not only in the deepest wilderness, but also along the fringes of civilization. I often kept my garage door open in winter to allow the ermine access, thereby using the natural method of rodent control. I found fresh ermine tracks entering my garage nightly, and it was not unusual to look out the window and see one bounding over the snow while coming or going.

The smaller short-tailed weasel is the most populous species, with the larger long-tailed species comprising only about a fifth of the total ermine population. In the lower reaches of the southern Rockies, biologists note that the long-tailed weasel is often missing.

Mating

Ermine breed in mid-March. How this happens is a miracle, as anyone who has ever seen the ferocious battles of two weasels meeting will attest. My guess is that the larger male subdues the female and holds her down long enough to mate her. As soon as she is released, the female runs off and never looks back.

Kits are born about forty days later, eyes closed and virtually hairless, except for a tiny tuft of mane along the back of the neck. The female lines her nest with the fur of mice and other prey animals. Eldon Percival, a rancher living near Burritt's Rapids, Ontario, wrote, "We were removing hay from a corner of the barn one morning when a highly agitated weasel began hopping back and forth. I guessed that we'd disturbed a female's den, so I investigated. As I peeled back layers of hay, I discovered a very cozy den about the size of a water pail lined with the soft fur of mice. But then, to my dismay, I also noticed orange fur and what was left of our pet kitten that had disappeared the week before."

An average ermine litter is about five to six kits. The female tenderly cares for her babies and nurses them until their eyes open. When the young weasels are strong enough to travel, they trail after their mother on her hunts until they are able to fend for themselves. On occasion a pair of weasels can be seen traveling together. This is probably a female with one of her half-grown young from the last litter who has not yet moved off on its own. Come breeding season next spring, the first male attracted to the female will chase off the youngster.

Jaguar

GHOST PREDATORS
OF THE SOUTHERN
ROCKIES

Dusk settled upon the high country desert south of Tucson, Arizona, in the waning hours of August 7, 2003. The infrared camera lashed to a live oak tree had a clear view of the isolated ravine choked with brush, cholla cactus, and cat's claw bushes bristling with wickedly curved thorns. In the past four months, the sophisticated camera had detected the heat of warm-blooded animals many times, and snapped photographs of wandering black bears and mountain lions, curious coyotes and bobcats—along with a few illegal aliens and drug smugglers.

But this was no ordinary camera. Neither was its location nor its mission. This was a ghost hunt. The camera had been installed months earlier to capture a ghost on film, and the experts believed this ravine was a prime place to find one.

At fifteen minutes before midnight, a pack rat hopped into view, but its body heat was below the level necessary to energize the infrared cell. Moments later a 4-foot-long diamondback rattlesnake slithered into view, tongue darting to and fro as the snake followed the heat trail of the doomed rodent. The cold-blooded serpent wiggled after the rat and out of view.

A Ghost Makes Its Appearance

At midnight the sensitive infrared cell suddenly energized in response to the presence of heat. Three javelinas nervously trotted off to the right, beyond the camera's field of view, and were gone. Seconds later, the infrared sensor detected heat to its left. The ghost had arrived.

The heat exuding from the ghost's massive body set off silent alarms inside the camera, and all systems readied for action. The ghost stepped warily into a small grassy opening and sniffed at the tracks of the javelina it was following.

The ghost started moving away, but stopped and turned back, its extraordinary senses suddenly alert. It glanced up at the camera and turned, anxious to get away from the suspicious apparatus. Suddenly, a brilliant light blasted through the night, and the ghost bolted into the brush. Too late. The camera had captured on film one of the true ghost predators of the southern Rockies.

Within days every newspaper in Arizona carried the photo of a young male jaguar, with a short caption. *USA Today* carried the story, as did several other large newspapers. Finally, the cat (ignore the pun) was out of the bag, and the rest of Arizona—indeed, the rest of the country—learned what state officials had suspected for several years: el Tigre, the jaguar, had returned to the American Southwest.

Exciting News from the Southern Rockies

The northern Rockies are considered the stronghold of true wilderness predators such as the grizzly, wolf, wolverine, and lynx, with the central and southern Rockies being little more than a massive desolate rock pile inhabited by rattlesnakes, scorpions, and a few nondescript critters. Nothing could be further from the truth. Sure, there is good news up north, with the expansion of grizzlies into some of their historic range and the reintroduction of the gray wolf, but all of the really exciting environmental news is currently down south.

In the southern Rockies, several jaguars have been sighted and pho-tographed, and two were bayed and treed by mountain lion hunters. The Mexican gray wolf, like its northern cousin, has also been reintroduced to Arizona and New Mexico. Interest and sightings of two other exotic wild cats—the ocelot and the jaguarundi, rarely seen north of the Mexican border—have also peaked. And then there is the mighty grizzly, another ghost predator of the southern Rockies. Has the great bear returned? Did it ever leave?

The Return of the Jaguar

The jaguar once roamed throughout the southwestern states of Texas, New Mexico, and Arizona as far north as the Grand Canyon. This large predator quickly ran into trouble with early settlers who invaded its domain when it preyed upon an occasional cow or horse. Records of jaguar kills go back as far as 1900. Following are just a few of the sixty-two historical reports concerning this big cat.

In 1902 a jaguar killed a cow in the Datil Mountains of New Mexico. The settler's wife discovered the kill and laced it with strychnine. A large jaguar was found dead near the cow carcass the next day. In 1906 in Ari-zona's Chiricahua Mountains, a female jaguar and two kittens were trapped by a bounty hunter. The female was killed for the bounty, and the two kittens were offered for sale. In 1912, near Prescott, Arizona, cowboys roped a jaguar and stoned it to death.

Scores of jaguar deaths from government agents who trapped and poisoned them also fill the rolls. The stories go on and on. Many of these jaguars were killed not because they were preying upon livestock—they were merely encountered by duck or deer hunters or seen "near" cattle. In other words it was shoot or poison all predators on sight, which was not only accepted, but expected, in those days.

The most devastating spate of jaguar killings occurred in a four-year span from 1961 through 1965 in Arizona. Four jaguars were killed by hunters, and one of them was an adult female killed near the Grand

Canyon. Until then, it was thought that only male jaguars wandered north in search of new territory. But the killing of the female proved that the jaguar could very well establish a breeding population north of the border once again if the animals were not shot on sight.

As a result the U.S. Fish & Wildlife Service placed the jaguar on the Endangered Species List, making it illegal to kill one, even if the jaguar was preying on livestock. Many naturalists believed this was too little too late. With much of the Southwest being developed and the dearth of sightings, it was the general opinion among wildlife biologists that the jaguar would never again be seen north of the Mexican border, let alone establish a breeding population.

Photo Evidence of the Jaguar

That all changed on the morning of March 7, 1996, when rancher Warner Glenn's hounds chased what he thought was a mountain lion up a sharp ridge in southern Arizona's Peloncillo Mountains 50 miles north of the border. When Glenn caught up with his baying hounds, he was stunned to see the big cat had spots. He'd brought to bay a jaguar.

In the recent past officials had viewed most purported jaguar sightings with a mixture of skepticism and chagrin. And you couldn't blame them. One alleged sighting of a black jaguar south of Tucson turned out to be a black Labrador.

But Glenn's sighting was different. This was the smoking gun that would electrify the wildlife world. And Warner Glenn knew it. He hurriedly photographed the large male cat so there would be no question that it was a jaguar. His photographs got everyone excited. The same year another mountain-lion hunter treed a jaguar and photographed and videotaped it. Since then, there has been a spate of jaguar sightings— some authenticated, some not.

The Jaguar Is Adaptable

The jaguar is not only habitating close to the Mexican border, as evidenced by recent sightings. A 2004 mule deer kill on the south rim of the Grand Canyon, roughly 400 miles north of the border, may have been the work of a jaguar. This is high coniferous forest; it's also cold country in winter, lending further proof that the jaguar is highly adaptable and willing to live anywhere there is an ample prey base. A firefighter near Show Low, Arizona, hundreds of miles north of the U.S.-Mexico border, reported seeing a jaguar while fighting wildfires in the summer of 2003.

Studies have shown that, unlike other sensitive predators, the jaguar is not picky about where it lives. This big cat has been spotted in semi-desert grasslands, Sonoran desert scrub, interior chaparral, dense cactus forest and woodlands, and high-country evergreen forests. If there are animals to kill and eat, the jaguar is happy. Wildlife experts have said that what is most critical for the jaguar's survival is to keep intact travel corridors, so the jaguar can roam freely from established populations in the Mexican state of Sonora, 130 miles south of the border. But most importantly, people must stop killing jaguars. The U.S. Fish & Wildlife Service considers this to be the number one priority for re-establishment of the jaguar in the Southwest. While the shooting has stopped in the United States, jaguars in Mexico, though also protected, have been routinely shot by ranchers because of the big cat's tendency to occasionally prey on livestock.

The good news is that this vicious cycle of shooting jaguars in cattle country may be changing, thanks to the work of a few dedicated individuals. Oscar Moctezuma, who is with the nonprofit organization, Naturalia, purchased a 10,000-acre ranch in the heart of jaguar country in Mexico. Naturalia is committed to conserving the jaguar and other endangered species in the area, and raised the funds to purchase the ranch by selling silver coins with endangered species printed on them. This is the first parcel of land obtained in Mexico specifically to protect jaguars.

Jaguar researcher Carlos Lopez Gonzales has been studying the cats on this ranch for the past few years. He has collared a few mountain lions, and in March 2003, captured his first jaguar, a lactating female, which he radio-collared and released. Signals from the collar show that the female is staying in the area, an indication she has kittens nearby.

Another researcher, Raul Valdez, has been working in the same area with landowners who control 74,000 acres of prime jaguar habitat. Though these ranchers lose ten to twenty head of livestock each year to jaguar depredation, they have decided they will no longer kill the offenders. These landowners have also removed most of the cattle from this area. They have come to realize that the jaguar is a precious commodity, not only as a wildlife resource, but also as a way of regrouping financially. The possibility exists that if jaguar numbers increase, limited sport hunting may be allowed.

This may sound contradictory, but it should be remembered that most jaguar habitat in Mexico is under private ownership, and for the jaguar to flourish to the point where surplus animals migrate north to establish breeding populations, some concessions must be made for the overall good of the species. This conundrum is put into clearer perspective when the ramifications of unregulated jaguar killing are closely examined. Recently, two jaguars were killed in this area; one was a breeding-age female. With regulated hunting, this female would have been allowed to escape.

Jaguar Facts

The jaguar is a large, powerfully built cat and has no natural enemies save man. An adult male may weigh upwards of 250 pounds, and a female about 150 pounds. Forest jaguars tend to be a bit smaller than open-country cats, no doubt because the jaguars who hunt in open country stalk larger prey. The jaguar's head is large and its jaws are powered by massive balls of muscles that allow it to kill even large animals with a single bite to the head.

A jaguar's prey includes anything it can catch and eat. That may be fish, turtles, and large caiman in the rainforest rivers, or monkeys and marsh deer on the ground. In the Cockscomb Basin Reserve in Belize, the predominant prey is the armadillo. This animal's bony armor frustrates all predators but the mighty jaguar, whose powerful jaws are able to penetrate it. In Mexico and the southwestern United States, the jaguar hunts javelina and Coues (a smallish subspecies of white-tailed deer), along with mule deer, raccoons, coati mundi—and virtually anything else that moves.

The jaguar's coat is a thing of beauty—and function. Its pale yellowish coat is festooned with black rosettes, creating the ideal jungle camouflage. In densely forested areas the jaguar's coat tends to be darker, but in open areas its coat is lighter. Melanistic, or black jaguars, are common in some areas.

Unfortunately, the jaguar's coat of many colors was also admired by the fashion industry. The jaguar began a serious decline in the 1960s and '70s when much of the South American rainforests were logged, and unregulated hunting of jaguars for their pelts resulted in almost 18,000 jaguar deaths every year. Today, there are an estimated 15,000 jaguars remaining in South, Central, and North America.

One of the most potentially damaging programs to the return of the jaguar is a megalithic barricade proposed by the U.S. Department of Immigration that would run the full length of the 351-mile-long border between Arizona and Sonora, of which 261 miles would be in the Tucson sector. This steel and concrete structure would effectively stifle the flow of jaguars between breeding populations in Sonora and the southwestern states. Also added to this barrier would be stadium lights and about 631 miles of new roads in the Tucson area alone.

It doesn't take a jaguar expert to figure out that this structure would be a sure cat killer. Fortunately, Jim Caffey, director of the U.S. Border Patrol, is a level-headed man. He admits the agency "got a little carried away." After much protest from human rights and environmental groups this entire program is being scaled down—even rethought. Let's hope so.

The Mexican Wolf Is Back—Sort Of

The story of the Mexican wolf is in some ways similar to its northern cousin, the gray wolf. Yet it is also unique and more tragic. Like the gray wolf, the Mexican wolf was villainized and demonized when it began preying on the cattle sent into the arid grasslands of the Southwest by large cattle companies that had taken over the land after the Indians were removed. Do we see a pattern here? The frustrating thing about this scenario is that historians remind us the Mexican wolf was not in abundance in the Southern Plains back in the mid-1800s, when the first big cattle companies moved in.

Nature made the Mexican wolf smaller and faster than the gray wolf. A mature male Mexican wolf, at fifty to eighty pounds, is dusky gray and looks like a cross between a coyote and a gray wolf. This wolf inhabited mountainous country much of the year, hunting the fleet mule and Coues deer, and the javelina, but when it migrated to the lower country in winter, it found droves of dim-witted, slow-moving animals that would not even run away.

In response to cattle lost to the wolves, ranchers began a program of genocide that to this day ranks as one of the most wanton slaughters of wildlife. A survey in 1850 reported that all ranchers along both sides of the Mexican border were lacing fresh livestock kills with strychnine. A devastating drought in 1893 killed almost 70 percent of the cattle in the Southwest, and these piles of rotting carcasses brought scores of wolves down from the mountains to feast on beef—and to acquire a taste for it.

In 1907 the U.S. Forest Service got involved in wolf poisoning and killed hundreds of Mexican wolves in Arizona and New Mexico. Then the U.S. government officially joined the slaughter when it formed the Predatory Animal and Rodent Control (PARC) Agency. Government hunters and trappers spread out through the Southwest and trapped and poisoned every predator in their path. In 1923 alone PARC hunters "treated" thirteen million acres in Arizona. Besides eradicating untold millions of predators besides wolves, poisons also killed off the thin resident population of jaguars, as evidenced by reports, thereby ensuring the demise of a resident breeding population of this magnificent cat.

If one thing can be said in favor of PARC, it was one of the few efficient government agencies. By 1925 Mexican wolves were mostly gone from the United States, with the exception of a few holdouts in isolated mountain ranges. However, wolves from Mexico continued to cross the border to inhabit range devoid of competition, but by 1950, the Mexican wolf was even disappearing across old Mexico.

By 1960 sightings of Mexican wolves were rare. In 1970 the last Mexican wolf was shot in Texas, the last one in Arizona in 1975, and the last one in New Mexico in 1976. Officially, the Mexican wolf was extinct in the southwestern United States. Still, a very small population existed in Mexico. Amazingly, some far-sighted people sent professional trapper Roy McBride into this wilderness in 1980, where he live-trapped five of the last known Mexican wolves. These wolves entered into a captive breeding program that today has yielded about 175 Mexican wolves.

That's how close the Mexican wolf came to extinction. Or did it? McBride stated that in his opinion there were maybe another fifty wolves strung out through this vast region. Occasional sightings of "ghost wolves" have persisted in Mexico and the Southwest through the years. Of course, they were all discounted.

The reintroduction of the gray wolf to the northern Rockies has garnered much of the "wolf news," not only because of its success, but also because of its acceptance by many residents in the states of Montana and Idaho. The same process of analyzing and then implementing a plan for the reintroduction of the gray wolf was also carried out for the reintroduction of the Mexican wolf to the southern Rockies. Essentially, the U.S. Fish & Wildlife Service found ample habitat suitable for the long-term survival of Mexican wolves.

A program—including who, when, where, and how—for returning the Mexican wolf to its historic haunts was implemented. From the beginning the program lacked the smoothness of its northern counterpart. The best part was the "who." Unlike the northern reintroduction, which used

Canadian wolves trapped and shipped south, the southern program used Mexican wolves from the remnant populations held in captivity. These Mexican wolves were true (as per DNA testing) blood relatives of Mexican wolves that had been roaming wild and free just three decades earlier.

Certain wolves that exhibited wildness and independence were sent to isolated enclosures near carefully chosen release sites, where they were fed deer and elk carcasses to acclimate them to the natural prey base. The initial release sites were located in the Blue River Range, a vast expanse of 1,032 square miles of prime wolf habitat in eastern Arizona's Apache National Forest. On March 29, 1998, the acclimation pens were opened and the first Mexican wolves tentatively stepped forward.

Three packs quickly established themselves. A male and female, known as the Turkey Creek Pack, roamed freely for barely a month before the "Southwest Solution" to wolf problems reared its ugly head. The male wolf was shot and killed by a camper when the wolf attacked a dog at a campsite (wolves establishing territory routinely contest the presence of a competitor).

There has ensued an ebb and flow of the Mexican wolf in the seven following years. Today, the gray wolf up north has blossomed and numbers almost a thousand, but the Mexican wolf in 2005 stands at about twenty-five, depending on how many have been shot and killed since the last official count. This problem continues even though the U.S. Fish & Wildlife Service and other conservation organizations offer rewards as high as $100,000 for information leading to the arrest of anyone killing a Mexican wolf.

True, there have been a few wolf killings up north as well, but most of those people were swiftly brought to justice. In the Southwest, it's different. As in silence. I believe the proclivity of people in the Southwest to shoot wolves introduced by the government is a sign of the mistrust they have for most government activity. Up north, federal foresters, fish biologists, landscape architects, and even rangers are in constant contact with the people who live there, and they are generally trusted as friends and co-workers of the land. One of my best friends is Rob Garner, ranger for the Superior District in the Lolo National Forest. Depending upon the issue, I routinely contact Rob to agree, help, encourage, correct, disagree, and complain. And the wonderfully refreshing thing is he likes it!

These relationships are different in the southern Rockies. Federal employees are usually housed in isolated outposts, and some say any contact with the public is more of a "You can't do that" type of communication. Hence, there is a SSS (shoot, shovel, and shut up) approach by many (not all) residents in wolf country in Arizona and New Mexico.

Interestingly, some of these radio-collared wolves have been seen in the company of wolves without radio collars. Where did they come from? Are they wolves that have shed their collars? Or are they "ghost" wolves, survivors that were tucked back in isolated canyons in the heart of the Blue River Range. Perhaps those few wolves remaining in Mexico were lured north by the beckoning howl of the Turkey Creek male before he was shot.

It's still a toss-up whether the Mexican wolf will survive. Wolves are still being shot. There's always, it seems, a list of rewards being offered for one or more wolf killings. Old habits die hard in the Southwest, where established residents cling to their historical past with fierce pride.

Are these anti-wolf people evil? Absolutely not. Are they wrong to shoot wolves? Absolutely yes. I spent the winter of 2004 in the Southwest researching jaguar and wolf sentiment, and I found it curious that even the old-timers embraced the return of the jaguar. Yet, their trigger finger begins to twitch at the mention of wolves. I believe this is mostly due to a misguided fear that the federal government will step in right behind the red wolf reintroduction and start putting wolf country off-limits to these freedom-loving people.

I've had my best success with local residents in wolf country by helping them to understand that the Mexican wolf, even if it should number in the hundreds, would have a negligible impact on their lifestyles. Hunters need not fear that all their deer and elk will be killed, or worse, put off-limits. Ranchers need not fear that wolves will be allowed to kill their livestock with impunity.

Ignorance and fear are the cowards who kill the Mexican wolves as quickly as they trot onto the landscape. If you live in the Southwest, don't get into a spitting match with an anti-wolf person. Find out what they fear and agree with them that they have every reason to be fearful, then explain how a couple dozen Mexican wolves will not bring about the realization of their fears. I've used this tactic. It works.

The Ocelot Needs a Little Help

The ocelot is a smallish cat, weighing about forty pounds, with a long tail and chainlike black streaks along its tawny body, instead of spots (like the leopard), or rosettes (like the jaguar). The quickest way to tell the difference between an ocelot and a small jaguar is to look at the tail. A jaguar's tail is spotted; an ocelot's tail is not.

It is a little-known fact that a few ocelots were once found north of the border. Not many, though, because southern Arizona and New Mexico, along with western Texas, represent the northern limit of this cat's range. But they did exist there, with several sightings and a few killings occurring in these states. Texas today still has a small verified ocelot population.

It would not take much to return the ocelot to these areas, if it doesn't already lurk in a few isolated ranges of dense cover. There's even some evidence that suggests this. Recently, an ocelot was shot in Mexico just 15 miles south of the border, and a breeding population exists only 130 miles south of the border.

The wonderful work being done by pioneering biologists to educate Mexican citizens and ranchers about the benefits of the jaguar may pay off with the ocelot. If fewer of these fascinating cats are shot within a hundred miles of the U.S. border, it may be only a matter of time before ocelot sightings rival those of the jaguar.

The U.S. Fish & Wildlife Service is currently drafting a recovery plan that proposes to reintroduce the ocelot to a few select areas, such as the vast chaparral brush fields of west Texas and eastern New Mexico and the dense woodlands of southern Arizona. These places have a healthy bobcat population. Why not the ocelot also? It's not like we're trying to force a square wildlife species into a round habitat hole. This was all once ocelot range. Let's hope the ocelot returns to it, naturally or otherwise.

What the Heck Is a Jaguarundi?

Don Donaldson knows jaguarundis intimately; he once owned one. This smallish, twenty-pound subtropical cat, colored tawny or gray and unspotted, looks somewhat like a miniature mountain lion, though its slim, bullet-shaped head is unique. Don was given a jaguarundi by the owner of an exotic animal shop in Seattle when he worked for the U.S. Food and Drug Administration. For two years Don owned the cat and especially enjoyed when the jaguarundi went into hunting mode and stalked both his wife, Norma, and him throughout the house, then said hello with a heart-stopping leap onto their shoulders.

There have been more than a score of jaguarundi sightings reported in southern Arizona through the years, some by respected naturalists. Many others were discounted as unreliable, usually because biologists doubted that the people knew a jaguarundi from a house cat.

The most negative reaction to the question of the jaguarundi in Arizona comes from the respected biologist Carlos Lopez Gonzalez, who is studying jaguars in Sonora, Mexico. In a professional paper appearing in the *Arizona-Nevada Academy of Science Quarterly,* Gonzalez casts grave doubt on the existence of the jaguarundi north of the border. He mentions that through all of his trapping of cats on the ranch where he works, and from interviews with locals throughout Sonora, many jaguars, lions, and bobcats, and a few ocelot hides, skulls, and photos were produced. However, no one recalled ever having seen a jaguarundi.

Furthermore, Lopez Gonzalez states, no known record of a jaguarundi exists for Arizona, and the closest known breeding population of jaguarundis is 400 miles south of the border near Choix, Sinaloa. Given the limited range of the jaguarundi, which is about 16 square miles, Lopez Gonzalez believes it would be doubtful that a breeding female would ever venture so far north. He even sniffs at such reported sightings as wistful and unprofessional.

But back to Don Donaldson. If anyone knows jaguarundis it is Don. As we sat in a diner in Lake Havasu City, Arizona, one hot spring day, he recounted an incident that occurred several years back while he was driving towards the town of Portal, Arizona, 50 miles north of the border to view the many colorful subtropical birds that migrate north beginning in late spring.

Don told me, "Norma and I were driving along an isolated road in the Turkey Creek drainage west of Portal just after dark, when this animal trots onto the road 30 yards away and stops, probably blinded by my car's headlights. One look and I knew immediately what it was. I was about to jostle my sleeping wife's shoulder and say, 'Norma, wake up! There's a jaguarundi in the middle of the road.' But before I could, the jaguarundi scampered into the brush. If someone wants to call me a liar, that's their business, but I know what I saw. It was the same animal I lived with for two years."

As Carlos Lopez Gonzalez affirms, there has never been concrete evidence of a jaguarundi in Arizona, such as a carcass or photograph, to authenticate the presence of this animal. Lopez Gonzalez even discounts a sighting in Sonora by a herpetologist because, as he notes, the guy had been up for quite a while and must have been tired. Hmm! And yet, reports continue to filter in, some of which are admittedly highly questionable. Then there's Don Donaldson's sighting. And there's also a story by Arizona state Nongame Mammal Program Manager Bill Van Pelt, who told me that he knows a mountain-lion hunter who swears his hounds have chased jaguarundis in the Fort Huachuca, Arizona, area. In fact there have been more than a dozen recent sightings reported from this area, prompting state wildlife officials to install infrared cameras.

All of which leads to a delicious question. "Could there be a trace population of jaguarundis tucked back in the dense woodlands or cactus forests of southern Arizona or the mesquite/chaparral thickets of west

Texas or eastern New Mexico? And if not, could/should state or federal wildlife agencies introduce an experimental population?

A Tiny Cat Called Margay

A margay is a smallish ten-pound subtropical cat with bulging brown eyes and a body so long and leggy the animal looks like it is starving. The margay's tail is long and bushy and drags on the ground; its tawny fur is patterned with thick-edged rosettes and long ovals.

This cat once was native to the Southwest. A specimen shot near Eagle Pass, Texas, in 1852 stands as irrefutable proof. The question today is whether any margays still exist in the dense mesquite/chaparral thickets in Texas or thornscrub jungles elsewhere. There certainly hasn't been any proof in recent times. Is the margay extinct north of the Mexican border? Should it remain so?

Some respected biologists become irritated by the mere mention of the margay, claiming that lay people such as myself are meddling in environmental issues that smack more of wishful thinking and sensationalism than biological fact. But I counter with the question that they really don't have an acceptable professional answer for this question: If the margay (or the jaguarundi or the ocelot) was once native to certain areas of the Southwest, shouldn't state and federal wildlife agencies consider bringing it back?

My case revolves around the environmental holocaust wrought by the thirty million acres in the Southwest treated with strychnine for several decades beginning in the mid-1880s. This unprecedented event resulted in thousands of documented poisonings of wolves, grizzlies, jaguars, ocelots, mountain lions, and bobcats, as well as jaguarundis in Texas. Though undocumented, there surely were margays also poisoned. So why not right a wrong? Why not reintroduce the margay into a few select areas of mesquite/chaparral in Texas, where it once survived by catching mice, rats, and an occasional opossum, as its cousin, the bobcat, presently does? Maybe even reintroduce it to the scrublands in southern New Mexico and Arizona.

Ghost Grizzlies

The afternoon sun had warmed the high country forest as Colorado out-fitter Ed Wiseman led his elk bowhunting client down a narrow ridge in the south San Juan Mountains in September of 1979. The sun would soon dip below the horizon and a brisk September chill would once again envelop the landscape.

The bull elk were in the rut and their musical bugles echoed off the surrounding mountains. Ahead, a bull bugled, and the men moved cautiously forward. The hunter spotted a slumbering bear off to his left and stalked over for a look. It was a brownish bear, curled up on frost-burnt grass, snoring loudly. The hunter was after elk, not a bear, so he slowly backed away.

The men circled around the bear and continued down the ridge. Ed Wiseman had seen many brown-colored black bears in the San Juans. He had never even entertained the thought that the bear might be a grizzly. Why should he? The great bear had been exterminated three decades earlier in Colorado. That was the official word of the Colorado Division of Wildlife. No grizzlies, period. Still, if anyone should have doubted the "no grizzly" edict, it would have been Ed Wiseman. He'd had previous clients, experienced hunters, who'd seen plenty of grizzlies while in Alaska. And a few of these men had sworn to Ed they had seen grizzlies and their tracks while hunting out of his camps in the San Juans.

Last of the Grizzlies

Like the jaguar and the wolf, and just about any other predator that so much as licked a strychnine-laced carcass, the grizzly throughout the Southwest was brought to the brink of extinction by this infamous white powder. Historical records show that the last verified grizzly kill in New Mexico was in 1930 by George Evans in the Black Mountain country west of Magdalen. Reports and unverified kills have continued through the decades.

The most striking report came in 1958 from Dr. Douglas Jester of New Mexico State University in Las Cruces. Jester claimed to have repeatedly seen a silver-tipped grizzly rummaging through a garbage dump with several black bears near Lake Malloy east of Raton near the New Mexico/Colorado border. Though this bear was observed eighteen times, no one from either state wildlife department bothered to investigate. Finally, this bear was killed by a Colorado game warden.

The last verified grizzly killing in Arizona occurred on September 13, 1935, when Richard Miller shot a three-year-old, 300-pound bear near Red Mountain northeast of Clifton in the bottom of Stray Horse Canyon. A year later, three experienced hunters encountered a bear in the same area with all the distinguishing characteristics of a grizzly. Then in 1939, another "last grizzly" was shot on the slopes of Mount Baldy.

In Colorado alone, PARC trappers poisoned, shot or trapped a whopping 5,148 bears. Still, Colorado's Rocky Mountains are so remote and rugged that through the years an occasional grizzly would emerge from its backcountry lair, only to be smarmily shot and hailed as "the last grizzly." Officially, the state claimed that a female grizzly killed in 1952 was the last grizzly within its borders. But every year, a few folks insisted they'd seen a grizzly here and there. These sighting were quickly discounted by state wildlife officials without even a cursory investigation. And why not? There were no grizzlies in Colorado.

Unfortunately, Ed Wiseman did not know that state officials were wrong about there being no more grizzlies in the southern San Juans as led his hunter down the ridge. He heard snapping behind him and turned, expecting to see a lovesick bull elk trot into the small opening above. Instead, Wiseman was startled to see a large brown bear galloping at him, bellowing in rage. He later stated that he believed the bear was startled awake when it caught human scent. Instantly, he knew it was a grizzly. Ed faced the charging bear and tried to use his bow to ward off the furious animal, but the bear knocked him flat.

The bruin tore at his leg, then grabbed his shoulder and shook him. Ed grabbed an arrow and jabbed the bear in the neck. To his amazement, the bear left him and walked a short distance before lying down. In a few minutes it was dead.

Contrary to what state wildlife officials had been claiming for thirty years, the grizzly had not been absent from the state of Colorado. It sure as heck wasn't absent from the ridge Ed Wiseman had hiked down. State wildlife officials were quick to correct themselves and admitted they had been wrong. There had been one grizzly left, but now it was dead and there were no more.

The public outcry from the Ed Wiseman incident forced the state to send a crew into the south San Juan Mountains for two summers. They found no concrete evidence, such as hair or visual sightings. However, terrestrial biologist Tom Beck, who led the expeditions, stated that there was some circumstantial evidence, such as very large tracks and massive digs, a telltale sign of grizzlies burrowing for marmots.

Still, sightings from reliable sources have continued through the years, including several sighting of grizzly bears, grizzly tracks, and hair samples that were tested and proven to most likely have come from grizzlies. Upping the ante, the Colorado Division of Wildlife stated that only specific evidence would be accepted as definitive proof of a grizzly: A carcass (such as the bear Ed Wiseman killed); a track positively identified as a grizzly paw print by a grizzly bear expert; photographs from an expert; or DNA evidence from cells taken from an animal. Frustrated bear people complained that they'd already furnished irrefutable proof with Wiseman's grizzly—why wasn't that enough?

Enter Doug Peacock, an outspoken grizzly bear advocate and the author of the book *Grizzly Years*. Spurred on by Wiseman's grizzly kill and several possible grizzly sightings, Doug led an expedition to find and return with evidence of the existence of grizzly bears in the San Juans during the summers of 1990-91. Though neither expedition produced a confirmed sighting (several times they encountered large brown bears in dense cover) or a photo or plaster cast of a grizzly track, the searchers discovered recent dig-ups, which are places where grizzlies scoop out huge mounds of dirt when digging for ground squirrels and marmots. They also returned with long brownish strands of bear hair, which were examined at a laboratory and determined to be compatible with grizzly hair.

Encouraging, but not exactly proof positive of the existence of grizzlies, especially since some state officials openly wondered if the brown hairs had been planted.

Colorado officials maintain their belief that there are no more grizzlies in the San Juan Mountains, and there are no plans to reintroduce bears. Doug Peacock and other bear enthusiasts have grudgingly moved on, taking the stand that they believe a few grizzlies still exist in the San Juans, but those last grizzlies will probably live out their lives in quiet isolation until they finally prove the state of Colorado correct.

In my opinion, a remnant population of grizzly bears still roam the San Juan Mountains of Colorado. The proof's been submitted; it just hasn't been acknowledged. I've also roamed much of the Rocky Mountains in this state, and believe me, there are many miles of rugged wilderness suitable for the great bear. The big problem, as I see it, is priorities. Colorado's Division of Wildlife exists as a giant elk factory, furnishing many millions of dollars to the coffers of private business and state agencies from elk hunters. It would throw a wrench into the gears of this giant machine to start messing around with grizzly bears. The grizzly was once, and may still be to some extent, part of nature's cycle in Colorado's Rockies. It would be arrogant and unprofessional to pick and choose which animals are the most economically efficient to nurture.

A Colorado official once asked me why I believed that there were still grizzlies living in the San Juans, since I admitted that I hadn't ever been in those mountains. I replied, "Ed Wiseman's dead grizzly was a female, and a necropsy proved that she'd borne young. So there had been offspring, probably several. And most assuredly there had been a boar to mate her. Where were they?"

The Mexican Grizzly

As late as 1956 the grizzly, occasionally referred to as "oso grande," lived in most mountainous parts of its historic Mexican range. That same year a taxidermist in Chihuahua had a live grizzly in his possession, the bear having been captured as a cub. And in 1957 naturalist Starker Leopold examined the skin of a large male grizzly killed by Isaias Garcia in Canon de Madre. That same year Garcia also killed a female in the same area. So we know that there were grizzlies roaming the Mexican Rockies in the late 1950s.

Tracks and other signs were found by research biologists for the next few years in several areas of the Sierra Madres, and in 1960 a ranch owner reported that a large grizzly had killed one of his cows. When another cow was killed in the area, poison was brought in and no grizzlies have been heard of since. And even though the grizzly had been placed on the list of protected animals in Mexico, poisoned carcasses were put out to kill them during the winters of 1961–1964 in the Sierra del Nido Mountains of Sonora. There is little doubt the last grizzlies were exterminated in this area by these clandestine poisoning programs.

It gets worse. In 1973 naturalist Stephen Johnson reported that a rancher along the Chihuahua/Sonora border had told him that there were maybe several dozen grizzlies in the area, and that they were holding their own. But then something happened. In 1974 Dr. Bernardo Villa, former director of wildlife for Mexico, gave a talk at the Chihuahua Desert Symposium on the status of the Mexican grizzly. Villa stated that eight grizzlies were reported poisoned by ranchers in the Sierra del Nido during the winter of 1973–1974. Villa mentioned that in 1971 he and an associate had visited the area and found signs of ten grizzlies in the area, but that now they were all gone. Old habits, it seems, die hard.

Is the grizzly gone from Mexico? Dr. Charles Jonkel, director or the Border (U.S./Canada) Grizzly Project, brought a research team to Sonora in 1977 and after exhaustive study, Jonkel concluded that there was strong evidence that grizzlies were present in remote areas of the Rockies where human intrusion was slight. During this study, a University of Montana wildlife student participating saw a grizzly in the central Sierra del Nido Mountains. And just across the border in Arizona, student researchers found an 11¾-inch track, far too large to have come from a black bear. Rumors persist, but no one in the United States or Mexico has shown much interest in bringing the Mexican grizzly back.

Making Things Right in the Southwest

Tens of millions of dollars have been spent on grizzly bears and gray wolves in the northern Rockies. It didn't bankrupt the federal government, nor the states involved, and it righted some environmental wrongs of the previous two centuries. The gray wolf and the grizzly up north are healthy and slowly moving into more and more of their ancestral ranges every year.

Why not attempt the same for the southern Rockies? A few pockets of wolves and grizzlies in Mexico, New Mexico, Arizona, or Colorado wouldn't annihilate deer and elk herds or force ranchers into insolvency. Neither would a few jaguars. And wouldn't it be exciting to catch a jaguarundi in the headlights of your car as you drove along a country road near Portal, as Don Donaldson had? How about seeing a dainty ocelot bounding away from a thicket as you hike along a trail in the Peloncillo Mountains? Or a tiny margay scrambling into a chaparral thicket at your approach?

Some biologists, at this point, might be heading for the proverbial soap box to preach the gospel of native species only for the Southwest. Let's set that record straight. Much of the wildlife revenue for the states of New Mexico and Arizona is carried on the back of a nonnative species introduced to these states in the early 1900s, the Rocky Mountain elk. Ranchers and market hunters had sent the native Merriam elk to extinction by the late 1800s. Wise naturalists eventually managed to haul some elk from Yellowstone to these states, and the results have been a spectacular success.

Sure, this reintroduction talk is all just a dream. Just like the dream of a gray wolf one day howling from a high ridge in Idaho, or a grizzly digging for marmots in Wyoming. Today, those dreams have taken form and become reality. And so can the dreams of bringing back many of the predators that were poisoned into actual or virtual extinction in the Southwest. Call it righting a wrong.

CONCLUSION

In a perfect world there would be no right or wrong. All plants and animals, fishes and fowl, men, and women, would live in harmony on this earth. Somebody even wrote a song about it called, "The Age of Aquarius."

You don't need me to tell you we're not there yet. Far from it, especially when it comes to nature, for that which was once natural has been changed to conform to man's needs, sometimes gently, more often brutally.

From day one the Pilgrims struggled mightily to wrest civilization from the wilderness with muscle and musket. In those precarious times, there wasn't a Pilgrim alive who would feel a pang of guilt to lay the bead of his flintlock on a wolf or panther that was nosing around his livestock pen.

And lest we of this present "enlightened" age be so pompous as to suggest we'd rather starve than kill an innocent wild animal, consider the following. A survey was taken that posed the question, *if you had to kill something to survive, would you do it?* The answer was an overwhelming Yes! Under circumstances of dire emergency, such as starvation, even the vegetarian admitted that he or she would kill to survive.

We need only look at the desperate situation the members of an Argentinian soccer team found themselves in after their airplane crashed on a remote, snow-choked mountainside in the Andes Mountains. With no hope of rescue after two weeks, more than a score of young men faced sure death unless they addressed some very uncomfortable issues: What would they do to survive? Trapped in the frigid hull of their wrecked ship in 10 feet of snow, with dead bodies all around them, they were forced to think the unthinkable. To survive, they had to eat the flesh of teammates who had died. What followed was a heartbreaking, yet sobering, tale of what human beings will do to survive.

Some of those hearty adventurers, the pioneers and settlers who first ventured south and west into the wilderness called Kentucky, and later across the Mississippi and up the Missouri, and eventually across the vast sea of buffalo grass we now call the Great Plains became the nucleus of our country's heroes. Daniel Boone, Davy Crockett, Meriwether Lewis and William Clark, Jim Bridger—all share a special niche in the rich early history our nation. But they did it by conquest, by the flash of their muskets, as Captain Clark recorded grizzly kill after grizzly kill in his diary during the Lewis and Clark Expedition of Discovery.

Those Pilgrims, pioneers, settlers, ranchers, and farmers of yesteryear were not evil people seeking to drench the land with as much wolf and bear blood as they could. They were desperate, frightened people who were ignorant of the delicate balance of nature in the land they furtively trod. I believe that most of us today would have done the same thing back then: trapped animals for their furs, shot the wolf in the corral, bludgeoned to death the ermine in the chicken coop. Anything to keep our loved ones alive. It's called the law of the jungle—survival of the fittest. And now we're the supreme predator at the top of the food chain. So, obviously, we won.

Or did we?

True, our country has experienced a cornucopia of material blessings unlike anything seen in the annals of history. Extraordinary isn't a good enough word to describe what we've wrought from this once-untamed wilderness in just a few centuries. Yet if we look at America as a nationwide ecological machine, it doesn't take much probing to see that it is out of tune, that it is leaking oil—a sign of wear. But you don't throw the engine away when it leaks a little oil. Fix it and it'll keep purring right along.

Environmentally, that's what America needs to do. In creating the superb economy and society of today, we've worn out some of the land and its inhabitants. The naysayers like to cry doom and gloom over the state of the environment. I personally have no patience for the negative—too much time and energy spent on stating the obvious, rather than fixing it.

Yes, we've done some (many?) things wrong environmentally in the Rocky Mountain West while carving out an exceptional nature-oriented society that is the envy of the much of the urbanized world, as evidenced by the steady stream of newcomers who move to the Rocky Mountain states every year.

Where to from Here?

The environmental devastation wrought by the PARC hunters and trappers can be righted. Strychnine, even with its macabre afterlife of six years, eventually erodes to nothing. Nature has a way of healing itself, but sometimes it needs help. True, God formed the animals from the dust of the earth, but that was a one-time thing. We can't expect Mother Nature to repeat this miracle. She needs our help to bring back the ocelot or the Mexican grizzly where there are none.

We can still right the ship environmentally. A perfect world? Naw! But we can endeavor to be good stewards of the land. Not like that crazy eastern professor who suggested the government move people out of the sparsely populated areas of the West in order to create a vast, pre-Lewis and Clark environment.

Instead, we can right the ship by becoming environmentally sensitive in our everyday lives. Not as eco-freaks who tie themselves to trees, but as rational human beings who fully understand that every square of toilet paper that we use to wipe our butts comes from a tree; that every time we flush a toilet, it impacts nature. We can make right and wrong decisions about the environment. And if we do make the wrong decision, we can go back and fix it—if not entirely, then at least to the best of our ability.

That's what's happening in the northern Rockies with the reintroduction of the gray wolf and the grizzly bear in areas where these predators had been absent for so long, and in the southern Rockies with the carefully monitored natural reintroduction of the jaguar. But that's yesterday's news. What about today? What about tomorrow?

BIBLIOGRAPHY

Books

Bass, Rick. *The Lost Grizzlies: A Search for Survivors in the Wilderness of Colorado.* New York: Houghton Mifflin, 1995.

———. *The New Wolves.* New York: Lyons Press, 1995.

———. *The Nine Mile Wolves.* New York: Mariner Books, 2003.

Brown, Davis E. *The Grizzly in the Southwest.* Norman, Okla.: University of Oklahoma Press, 1996.

Petersen, David. *Ghost Grizzlies: Does the Great Bear Still Haunt Colorado?* New York: Houghton Mifflin, 1995.

Rue, Leonard Lee III. *Sportsman's Guide to Game Animals.* New York: Outdoor Life Books, 1968.

Seton, Ernest Thompson. *Lives of Game Animals.* New York: Charles T. Bramford Company, 1953.

Periodical Articles

Devlin, Sherry. "Cattle-Killing Wolves in Ninemile Slated to Die." *The Missoulian*: August 6, 1998.

———. "Wolves Attack Another Llama at Ninemile." *The Missoulian*: April 3, 2002.

————. "Wolves Suspected of Llama Attacks Shot, Killed." *The Missoulian*: March 26, 2002.

Gadbow, Daryl. "Nine Mile Wolves Bite Again, Attacking Another Llama." *The Missoulian*: March 24, 2002.

Krajik, Kevin. "The Fugitive." *Audubon Magazine.* January/February, 1997.

Pitzl, Mary Jo. "Giving Mexican Wolf More Space." *Arizona Republic Newspaper* January 21, 2005.

Weller, Robert. "Lynx Fight for Life in Colorado." *The Missoulian*: June 13, 1999.

Research Paper

Jonkel, Charles. "Mexican Grizzly Studies." Published research paper by the Northern Border Grizzly Research Study. 1978.

ABOUT THE AUTHOR

Mike Lapinski is the award-winning author of twelve outdoor and nature books and hundreds of magazine articles. His wildlife photos have appeared as interior and cover art in a variety of magazines and books. Mike is also the host of numerous outdoor and nature video programs.

Mike is considered an expert on the use of bear pepper spray. He often speaks on this subject, and on bears, and self-defense for nature lovers. Mike lives with his wife, Aggie, in the heart of the Rockies in Superior, Montana.